March 16, 1993

May the Lord bless
you and keep you —
while we are absent
one from the other.
Your 8:30 A.M. Tuesday
Prayer Partners —

Lonnie Wascom
Ruby Cahler
Ruth P. Keen
Dorothy Guma
Opal Rae Wild

Layman's Bible Book Commentary
Mark

LAYMAN'S BIBLE BOOK COMMENTARY

LB BC

MARK

VOLUME 16

Johnnie C. Godwin

BROADMAN PRESS
Nashville, Tennessee

Dedicated to Mark, Larry, Steve

4211–86
ISBN: 0–8054–1186–0

Dewey Decimal Classification: 226.3
Subject heading: BIBLE. N. T. MARK

Library of Congress Catalog Card Number: 78–054774
Printed in the United States of America

Foreword

The *Layman's Bible Book Commentary* in twenty-four volumes was planned as a practical exposition of the whole Bible for lay readers and students. It is based on the conviction that the Bible speaks to every generation of believers but needs occasional reinterpretation in the light of changing language and modern experience. Following the guidance of God's Spirit, the believer finds in it the authoritative word for faith and life.

To meet the needs of lay readers, the *Commentary* is written in a popular style, and each Bible book is clearly outlined to reveal its major emphases. Although the writers are competent scholars and reverent interpreters, they have avoided critical problems and the use of original languages except where they were essential for explaining the text. They recognize the variety of literary forms in the Bible, but they have not followed documentary trails or become preoccupied with literary concerns. Their primary purpose was to show what each Bible book meant for its time and what it says to our own generation.

The Revised Standard Version of the Bible is the basic text of the *Commentary*, but writers were free to use other translations to clarify an occasional passage or sharpen its effect. To provide as much interpretation as possible in such concise books, the Bible text was not printed along with the comment.

Of the twenty-four volumes of the *Commentary*, fourteen deal with Old Testament books and ten with those in the New Testament. The volumes range in pages from 140 to 168. Four major books in the Old Testament and five in the New are treated in one volume each. Others appear in various combinations. Although the allotted space varies, each Bible book is treated as a whole to reveal its basic message with some passages getting special attention. Whatever plan of Bible study the reader may follow, this *Commentary* will be a valuable companion.

Despite the best-seller reputation of the Bible, the average survey of Bible knowledge reveals a good deal of ignorance about it and its primary meaning. Many adult church members seem to think that its study is intended for children and preachers. But some of the newer translations have been making the Bible more readable for all ages. Bible study has branched out from Sunday into other days of the week, and into neighborhoods rather than just in churches. This *Commentary* wants to meet the growing need for insight into all that the Bible has to say about God and his world and about Christ and his fellowship.

BROADMAN PRESS

Contents

Introduction:

The Gospel of Mark

Viewpoint

Commentary introductions are important because they help the reader to see the viewpoint of the commentary author and know something about what to expect in the commentary itself. Good commentary introductions are also important because they give the Bible book's setting for the reader and provide a context that tells the reader something about the book's author, date of writing, purpose of writing, readers, and other helpful information.

Some writers of commentaries write with as much certainty as if the Gospel events happened yesterday and they were there to record everything. Actually, the historical events and the writing of the Gospels occurred over nineteen hundred years ago. Whatever merit this commentary may have, it is only a commentary. The text is the Bible. The reader should study the Bible in standard and conversational translations and then turn to the commentary for what help it may offer.

This volume on the Gospel of Mark tries to be true to the design of the *Layman's Bible Book Commentary* as expressed in the foreword: "The Bible speaks to every generation of believers but needs occasional reinterpretation in the light of changing language and modern experience." Or, as others have said, "We need to put the faith of our fathers in the language of our children." With this conviction, I've tried to use *people talk* that everyone understands.

There are many different viewpoints about the Gospel of Mark. Commentaries that try to be comprehensive go into those viewpoints in detail. Because of the nature and size limitations of this commentary, the reader needs to understand that he has the author's viewpoint without a wide range of alternative viewpoints. The value of such an approach is that the reader can get information in a hurry. The danger is that the reader may accept the viewpoint without considering the alternatives. With that much background let's pinpoint what most people want to know in reading a commentary introduction and then look at some details that will provide more foundation for study of the Gospel of Mark.

Pinpoint

John Mark wrote the Gospel of Mark in Rome for Roman Christians about A.D. 65 to encourage them during their persecution.

Getting to Know John Mark

John Mark is accepted as the author of the Gospel of Mark. The earliest Greek manuscripts were anonymous, but earliest tradition and earliest writings outside of the Bible credit Mark as the author. Though scholars differ on much about the Gospel of Mark, they usually agree that John Mark is the author.

John translates his Hebrew name, and *Mark* translates his Greek name. *Marcus* is Latin. In those days it was common to use the Hebrew name at home and to use the Greek or Roman name in other settings. And it is interesting to notice that John Mark's identification gradually changed from John to Mark (see Acts 12:12,25; 13:5,13; 15:37,39; Col. 4:10; 2 Tim. 4:11; Philem. 24; 1 Pet. 5:13—which are all the N. T. references to John Mark).

Mark was the son of a woman named Mary (Acts 12:12). Since the Bible doesn't mention Mark's father, most commentators conclude that he was dead. Mark and his mother lived in Jerusalem, so Mark grew up where some of the most vivid scenes of his Gospel took place. Mark's mother was well off financially. She had a large house and a maid; these facts reflect something of the financial picture (Acts 12:12–13). Mark was a cousin to Barnabas (Col. 4:10). Besides these relatives, Mark had the friendship of two outstanding apostles: Peter and Paul.

Peter may have led Mark to faith in Jesus Christ; whether he did or not, he looked upon Mark as his spiritual son (see 1 Pet. 5:13). Paul couldn't do with Mark, but he couldn't do without him either. Mark had gone on the first missionary journey with Paul and Barnabas to serve as a helper (Acts 13:1–5). There is no reason to assume that Mark had to do the equivalent of shining shoes and carrying out the garbage—though he may have. More likely, he was helpful in training new converts and serving as personal secretary to Paul and Barnabas. For some reason, Mark left Paul and Barnabas at Perga in Pamphylia and returned to Jerusalem (Acts 13:13). Whatever the reason was, it led to the first known personality conflict within a foreign mission team (see Acts 15:36–40). Later Paul wouldn't agree to take Mark on another missionary journey, so Barnabas and Paul went in separate directions. Mark kept his missionary commitment and enthusiasm for sharing the gospel, and Paul learned the lesson of giving a second chance through his experience with Mark. Later, Paul counted on Mark to help him and obviously had a deep love for Mark (Col. 4:10; 2 Tim. 4:11; Philem. 24).

But it was undoubtedly Peter's influence that played such an important part in the content of Mark's Gospel. We'll look at that matter more closely in a moment.

Mark matured as he turned from missionary failure to devoted disciple. Mark had skills as a teacher, evangelist, theologian, and writer. He had a keen mind that could analyze and put facts together to give an accurate portrait of Christ. He had a good memory, but he lived in the present tense and matched gospel truths to current needs as he exercised his gift of a pastoral heart. He spoke in *people talk* that grammarians have criticized, but he communicated with a good vocabulary that didn't make people reach for a dictionary.

Mark may have died a martyr's death—as some tradition has it. Regardless of how he may have died, the most important thing he did while he was alive was to give us the Gospel of Mark. We can be grateful that God inspired Mark to put the good news in writing. There are some very good reasons why God inspired Mark to write his Gospel, so let's look at some of those reasons.

Why Mark Wrote His Gospel

The best evidence we have indicates that Mark wrote his Gospel in the decade of A.D. 60–70. And because of the world scene and the content of the Gospel of Mark, A.D. 65 seems to be the best single date to set forth as the time of the writing. What was happening then? Tradition says that Peter and Paul were dead as the result of martyrdom. Rome had burned in the summer of A.D. 64. Nero, the Roman emperor, was the culprit who had Rome burned; but to get himself out of trouble, he blamed the fire on the Christians. The Christians were horribly persecuted and murdered. Owning up to being a Christian was like agreeing to a death sentence. Their persecution paralleled the kinds of persecution Christ went through as described in Mark's Gospel. So Mark's presentation of Jesus as the Suffering

Servant Messiah (Isa. 53) and the cost of discipleship gave encouragement and a renewed call to unfailing commitment to the Christians of Rome. The Gospel of Mark probably came between the A.D. 64 burning of Rome and the A.D. 66–70 Jewish wars that saw Jerusalem destroyed in A.D. 70. Persecution stands out most as the immediate cause of Mark's writing. But there are other purposes that can be drawn out and that still apply today.

The apostles and other eyewitnesses to the life of Christ were dying out, and the world needed the gospel story in writing as a continuing testimony. The written Gospel would serve as a faithful substitute record in place of the living voices. Mark wrote to give a portrait of Jesus as the living Christ, who still faces every person and demands a personal decision from each individual. Mark would have agreed with John in saying, "These are written that you may believe that Jesus is the Christ, the Son of God, and that believing you may have life in his name" (John 20:31).

To itemize some of the purposes, Mark wrote to: (1) encourage persecuted Christians, (2) share the good news about Jesus with others, (3) focus on discipleship, (4) put facts into writing as eyewitnesses died off, (5) set the record straight and guard against error, (6) remind readers of Jesus' suffering and redemptive death, (7) present the person and power of Jesus, (8) prepare readers for the second coming of Christ and for the events before that time, and (9) show the responsibility all Christians have to share the good news with others. These are some of the most obvious purposes.

What kind of Gospel would these purposes produce? The answer to that question is *the kind of Gospel Mark gave us.* But, again, there is more to the answer; and we need to come to an understanding of what Mark's Gospel is.

Getting to Know Mark's Gospel

Mark wrote the first, shortest, and easiest of the Gospels to understand. He led the way in a new kind of writing when he penned "The beginning of the gospel of Jesus Christ, the Son of God" (Mark 1:1). *Gospel* translates the Greek word for *good news.* Gospels are not biographies in the truest sense of the term. They leave out much that would be included in any regular biography. For example, Mark did not begin with the birth or the ancestry of Jesus. He began with

Jesus as a grown man who had come as the Son of God to fulfill Old Testament prophecy. Similarly, each of the Gospels leaves out much that would be included in a regular biography. Instead of being biography, the Gospels are composed of preaching at its best that calls on people to say yes to Jesus and no to self.

Sources of the Gospel.—Peter was undoubtedly the source for most of Mark's Gospel. The development of the Gospel parallels the boundaries Peter stated in Acts 1:22 and the events Peter outlined in Acts 10:36–41. The earliest records we have tell us that Mark served as Peter's interpreter and recorded the events of Jesus' life as Peter remembered them. The reference to interpretation may mean that Mark translated Peter's Hebrew or Aramaic into Greek, the universal language of that day. Mark often gave the Aramaic term and then translated it for the Gentile (non-Jewish) readers. Mark also interpreted Jewish customs for the Gentile readers. So the Gospel of Mark echoes how Peter would have written: with urgency, frankness, color, power, conviction, and meaningful details. Besides the content that came from Peter, there is indication of Mark's own narration and the inclusion of gospel truths that had been spoken by others and now were being put into writing. Mark himself may have been an eyewitness to part of what he wrote. Regardless of Mark's sources of material, the Holy Spirit obviously used Mark's own personality in the writing.

Outlining the book.—Outlining the book of Mark is a matter that different commentators approach in different ways: chronologically, geographically, topically, and in other ways. None of the outlining is really completely satisfactory. This commentary largely follows the chapter divisions of Mark, but sometimes it follows logical breaks or transitions that cross chapter lines. I wanted to keep sections in relatively small units for each focus and for ease of understanding.

Geographically, though, Galilee and Jerusalem are two key words to remember. The Gospel of Mark falls into two major parts: Mark 1:1 to 8:26 and 8:27 to 16:20. The first part focuses on Jesus' ministry both within Galilee and outside Galilee. The second part focuses on Jesus' movement toward Jerusalem and his ministry there that climaxed with his death, burial, and resurrection. The central thrust of the entire book is Jesus' movement toward the cross and resurrection. While Mark's Gospel has to be appreciated for itself and what

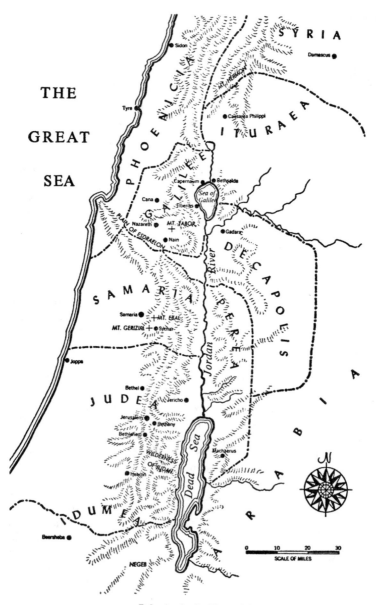

Palestine in the Time of Christ

it contains, I've drawn freely on the other Gospels for additional information about the events surrounding the final week of Jesus' life.

Another way of looking at the book of Mark is to say that chapters 1—9 show that Jesus came to minister, and chapters 10—16 show that he came to give his life. (See the table of contents for the breakdown of Mark into sections as this commentary deals with them.) For a traditional way of looking at the Gospel of Mark, consider the following outline:

I. Introduction: 1:1–13
II. Early Galilean Ministry: 1:14 to 3:6
III. Later Galilean Ministry: 3:7 to 6:13
IV. Ministry Outside Galilee: 6:14 to 8:26
V. Journey to Jerusalem: 8:27 to 10:52
VI. Ministry in Jerusalem: 11—13
VII. Passion (trial, suffering, death): 14—15
VIII. Resurrection: 16

Mark's special emphases.—Mark's Gospel has some special emphases that are interesting to point up. The Gospel emphasizes power. Over and over again we see the power of Jesus. He had power over demons, disease, death, nature, and any other obstacle that might hinder or threaten the will of God. Mark's Gospel focuses much more on miracles than on parables. The Romans were impressed with power, and Mark faithfully revealed the all-powerful Christ to the Romans.

The Gospel of Mark puzzles us with its record of Jesus' command to keep his messiahship secret. But then it helps us to see that the secrecy was to let Christ live in such a way that he would be shown to be God's kind of Messiah and not the sensational type of messiah that people would easily follow.

The theme of the kingdom of God dominates the Gospel of Mark, and we are able to see that the kingdom involves the will of God; but its meaning is still larger than we can understand. Besides the Roman persecution, non-Christian Jews hassled the Christians of Rome, the rest of Italy, and other places where Christians lived; and part of their problem was that they misunderstood the nature of Jesus' messiahship and the nature of the kingdom of God.

Mark's Gospel gives us a picture of Christ, and it leaves us wanting to know even more about him. These are just a few of the noble emphases that invite us to study and learn from Mark.

The Manuscripts of Mark

As far as we know, all our New Testament writings were first written in Greek (though some scholars believe part of the writings were first penned in Aramaic). None of the original manuscripts is available today. But the original manuscripts were soon copied, and we have ancient manuscripts that let us know we have what Mark wrote. The oldest manuscripts we have are naturally considered to be the closest to the original and also the most accurate. For example, Mark 16:9–20 is not in the oldest and best manuscripts; so these verses are not included in some translations. (See this commentary for further insights on these verses.)

Mark wrote in everyday Greek that was the language of the people. As mentioned earlier, his grammar has come under attack by various commentators who appreciate what Mark wrote but do not admire his use of Greek. Perhaps the grammar should take a backseat to the fact that Mark reached his goal of communicating. When he used an Aramaic term, he also gave its meaning in Greek. (Aramaic was closely related to Hebrew but different. Jews commonly used Aramaic instead of Hebrew in everyday speech.) When Jewish customs would not be familiar to Gentile readers, Mark explained the customs. He was a communicator.

Mark used the historical present over 150 times. In other words, he used the present tense to tell about past events. He presented the gospel in a way that causes the reader to feel that he was there when it happened. Mark wrote with urgency and in a way that calls for the reader to use all of his senses in receiving Mark's word pictures. Mark used the Greek word for *immediately* over forty times. He began two out of every three verses with *and*. He used the word for *again* twenty-five times. All of this says that Mark was excited about the gospel. That excitement came out in his writing and continues to be contagious today. No wonder Mark's Gospel holds such a high place today.

The Place of Mark's Gospel

The Gospel of Mark was more or less treated as the stepchild of the Gospels until relatively recent times. When it became evident that Mark was the first and primary Gospel, it was then moved to front and center of attention. Matthew and Luke had obviously had that kind of appreciation for Mark from the very beginning. Matthew has the essence of over 90 percent of Mark's verses, and Luke has the essence of over 50 percent of Mark's verses. The two Gospels often use Mark's actual words as they see things together with Mark. (Matthew, Mark, and Luke are known as the Synoptic Gospels, which means to see together.) Only thirty-one of Mark's verses do not appear somewhere in Matthew or Luke. And the Gospel of John probably has also drawn on Mark. These insights call us to a fresh appreciation of the Gospel of Mark.

Applying Mark's Gospel Today

The Gospel of Mark is vivid, stirring, and strong. These qualities fit the book to the restless, action-filled society of today. In our age people are looking for meaning, power, and freedom. So Mark has a special message for us today. The book reveals Christ as the one who has limitless power and the one who can guarantee freedom even over death. The Gospel shows us that the loudest cry of all was not "Crucify him!" Nor was it the cry of Jesus when he shouted, "It is finished!" The loudest shout was a shout of joy: "He is risen!" And through studying Mark's Gospel, each person can come to know the living Jesus personally and share in the promise of resurrection. Further, each person can find ways to live faith-filled lives of action for him. Now, it is time for "the beginning of the gospel of Jesus Christ, the Son of God" (Mark 1:1).

The Beginning of Good News
1:1–20

Starting Point of the Good News (1:1)

Mark's first verse offers the theme and summary of the book. "Beginning of the gospel" sums up the entire book and its events, for "gospel" means the announcing of the good news—not the predicting of it. To this point the gospel had been future; now it became present.

Mark was careful to identify the source of the good news: Jesus Christ. "Jesus" was a common Hebrew name that meant Savior. "Christ" was a Greek title that meant messiah (or anointed one) in Hebrew. Mark completed the title of his book with the term "Son of God"—a description of Jesus as the only begotten Son of God.

In different arrangements, each Gospel writer used the words Mark used; but only Mark combined the titles: Jesus, Christ, Son of God. If the Greeks had used punctuation marks, Mark likely would have put an exclamation mark after the title. So verse 1 really is the descriptive title of the book. However, the authorship title, "The Gospel of Mark," seems accurate also since scholars generally agree that Mark wrote the book.

Announcing the Good News (1:2–3)

Mark began the story with the God-inspired promise of the prophets Malachi and Isaiah. Compare Malachi 3:1 and Isaiah 40:3 with Mark 1:2–3. You will see why many Bibles list both prophetic passages here. Modern translations that are based on the best Greek manuscripts reveal that Mark credited Isaiah with both prophecies. The King James Version does not mention Isaiah; it simply refers to the "prophets" (v. 2). Scholars have not been able to find the first part of the quotation in Isaiah, but they have found it in Malachi 3:1. So the King James translation does away with the problem that some see in Malachi's not being mentioned. Mark was a Hebrew, and we might do well to comment further about the Hebrews' custom and about Mark's purpose. In quoting, the Hebrews were not concerned with scientific precision, and Isaiah was a major source who fit perfectly into the divinely inspired pattern of Mark's writing. Mark seems to have connected his thoughts primarily with Isaiah's, for Mark presented Christ in the same way as Isaiah: as the Suffering Servant. The main point is this: The good news of Jesus Christ came as a glad fulfillment of ancient Scriptures. And John the Baptist had the joy of announcing that good news.

Picturing the Good News in Symbol (1:4–5)

When John the Baptist appeared as the appointed messenger, his work was laid out for him. He was to make a road for the Lord, use preaching as his method, and tell people to prepare themselves for the divine coming. When a king traveled in those days, he sent workers to smooth the road and announce his coming. John had that job for the King of kings.

John was a Jew, and he began to do a strange thing to other Jews. When a Gentile (a non-Jew) wanted to become a Jew, he had to do three things: (1) get circumcised, (2) offer a sacrifice, and (3) be baptized. Circumcision is a relatively simple operation that involves cutting off skin from the front of the penis. For the Jews, circumcision symbolized both purification and a covenant between them and God. So a Gentile's circumcision identified him with the covenant people. The sacrifice was necessary to portray atonement for sins; it indicated both sorrow for past sin and an intention to turn from sin in the future. Sacrificing was a part of the Jewish way of life, and Gentile converts necessarily shared in sacrificing. Baptism was an immersion in water that symbolized a cleansing from the past life of sin and an entrance into the new life of Judaism. This act was required of Gentile converts, but baptism of Jews? There had been no such thing!

Yet, John, a Jew, plunged other Jews into the Jordan River when they repented and confessed their sins (v. 5). Jewish baptism was something brand-new. Jews were familiar with baptism all right, but only for people who were not Jews.

Nevertheless, every person needed the baptism that John offered. His baptism was an expression of repentance on the part of the one who abandoned his sins and confessed them openly.

Repentance usually means a change of mind; and although the New Testament usage of repentance carries that thought, the meaning goes even deeper. In the New Testament, repentance means coming to one's senses; it means a change of mind that shows up in a person's life through his beliefs, commitments, attitudes, and behavior. Quite simply, the repentant person has become born again. He was dead in his sins and trespasses, but now he is alive (Eph. 2:1,5). John the Baptist shared the news that everyone needed that experience.

Confession of sins accompanied baptism and repentance as a public facing up to one's sins. This public self-renunciation expressed through the mouth what had taken place in the heart; and the confession further qualified the individual for John's baptism. Multitudes of Jewish converts took the life-changing steps of repentance and confession. Then they welcomed John's baptism as a portrayal of their repentance and forgiveness. The total immersion pictured death and burial of the old way of living. Coming out of the water pictured entrance into a new kind of life. So baptism really is a testimony and a sermon in symbolic form.

Verse 5 does not mean that John literally baptized everybody in Jerusalem and Judea. It means, rather, that all types of people, in great numbers, came to John for baptism.

Fulfilling Prophecy (1:6–8)

John further fulfilled prophecy by arriving on the scene like an Old Testament prophet: His message was like Isaiah's, and his clothes were like Elijah's (2 Kings 1:8). John's food was locusts and wild honey. (Both were plentiful.) This description told of the customary way of life for Jesus' Forerunner.

One job of a slave was to untie the strap that held on his master's shoes. In effect, John was saying, "I am not fit to be the slave of the One mightier than I." So, in humble language, John announced that the Lord of lords was on his way (v. 7).

John drew a sharp contrast between his water baptism and Jesus' Holy Spirit baptism. John's water immersion was momentary, and it pictured the purified life of repentance. Jesus' Holy Spirit immersion would be eternal, and it would actually purify. Jesus would saturate his followers with his Holy Spirit.

Entering the Ministry (1:9–11)

Jesus presented himself for John's baptism even though Jesus was sinless and needed no baptism to picture his repentance. Then why was he baptized? Jesus counted himself a man, and he did everything

God expected a man to do. When John saw no reason to baptize Jesus, Jesus answered, "Let it be so now, for this is the fitting way for both of us to do our full duty to God" (Matt. 3:14–15, Williams). So in the event that signaled the beginning of his ministry, the divine Jesus identified himself with the sinful people he came to save. That was truly good news for mankind, and it's good news today.

The Spirit of God descended as Jesus was coming up out of the water. John the Baptist saw the Spirit's descent (John 1:32–34), and the voice of God the Father was audible (Mark 1:11). Spirit, Son, and Father—all three were present. The Spirit gave Jesus power for his ministry, and the Father voiced his delight with his Son's beginning ministry (compare Isa. 42:1). Jesus had reassurance of his divine mission and sonship. The good news had begun.

Overcoming the Adversary (1:12–13)

After the awesome and unique experience of his baptism, Jesus was sent by the Holy Spirit into the wilderness to be exposed to temptations that would test his purposes and methods. In that day a wilderness was generally regarded as the home of evil powers and a stronghold of the devil. Jesus probably went to the Judean wilderness.

While it was the Spirit who drove Jesus into the wilderness, Satan provided the temptations. He tested the Lord to try to make him fall. God allowed the testing so that Jesus could conquer other temptations that might threaten his messiahship—the essence of the good news. The temptations in the Judean wilderness were real; they actually happened. Satan was the adversary.

Verse 13 identifies the scene, the contestants, the spectators, and the helpers of the victorious Christ. With wild beasts as onlookers, Jesus and Satan battled in the deepest wilderness. The Spirit had given Jesus the power to win because victory at that point was essential for all other victories to come. And win Jesus did! His victory was a major step in establishing the good news. After Jesus had won, the angels came to minister to him.

Satan tempted Jesus to make him fall; he tempts us for the same reason. However, just as in the case of Jesus, God allows temptation to strengthen us, not to make us fall. And the same Holy Spirit who gave Jesus the power to win will give us power to win over temptation today. Although temptation is a lifetime battle, each victory prepares us to do something positive for God.

Preaching in Galilee (1:14–15)

After John the Baptist's arrest, Jesus began his Galilean ministry, preaching the good news that came from God. The world had waited and hungered for the words of verse 15: "The time is fulfilled, and the kingdom of God is at hand; repent, and believe in the gospel."

"Kingdom of God" means the kingly rule of God. At that time the rule of God was to be internal rather than external, over the hearts of people rather than over the military powers of the day. Somehow, the kingdom was both present (Luke 7:18–23; 10:23–24) and yet to come (Mark 14:25; Luke 11:2). The present and future aspects of the kingdom of God still puzzle us today. But for God to have his way with man is always good news, and Jesus announced that the time had drawn near.

The news demanded a response of repentance and belief in the gospel (Mark 1:15). "Believe" is the word of response that answers the question of how to receive the good news. "Believe" means to take Jesus at his word, to have faith in the good news, to exercise trust in the gospel. Christian belief is always more than intellectual understanding. It is head and heart belief.

Calling for Discipleship (1:16–20)

There was a lapse of time—but not a lapse of thought—between the incidents recorded in verse 15 and those recorded in verses 16–20. The context of repenting and believing was immediately succeeded by the context of leaving and following.

Jesus commanded Simon Peter and Andrew to follow him (v. 17). The brothers had followed Jesus earlier (John 1:35–42), but this call was to continuous discipleship. A disciple is a learner. Later, these disciples would be called apostles: those sent on a mission. But before they could become ambassadors for Christ, they needed to become students of Christ.

Since Peter and Andrew were fishing, it was natural for Jesus to express his call in this way: "Follow me and I will make you become fishers of men" (v. 17). It was like saying, "You will gather great numbers of people for the kingdom of God." What good news!

Jesus promised to enable his disciples to bring others under the kingly reign of God. Immediately Andrew and Peter followed Jesus.

James and John were mending nets (or possibly folding nets) to get them ready for use (v. 19). They left their nets, their ship, their hired hands, and their father—they left all—to follow Jesus. The words for "follow him" in the Greek text show a once-and-for-all determination to follow Jesus (v. 20). Their dedication was and is the only kind that is fit for the King of kings.

The two sets of brothers answered Jesus' challenge with changed hearts. Their change of heart brought them a new loyalty, a new security, and a new occupation.

The timeless good news appeared when Jesus entered his public ministry; and now, as then, it demands a verdict from the listener. Answering yes to Jesus calls for a willingness to leave everything and to risk everything.

Focusing on Persons
1:21–45

Public Ministry (1:21–28)

On every sabbath the Jews assembled for a synagogue service of prayer, Bible reading, and teaching. For three hundred years little that was new had happened at the synagogue. But things were about to change! Jesus had been baptized, empowered by the Holy Spirit for ministry, and openly commended by God the Father. He had victoriously undergone Satan's temptations in the wilderness. He had begun to gather some of his disciples, and now he was beginning his public ministry.

"Synagogue" was the Jewish counterpart of today's local house of worship or church. Any Jewish community with ten families or more was supposed to have its own synagogue, so synagogues were scattered throughout the land; and larger cities had several of these places of worship and religious education. The synagogue had several officers but not a permanent preacher. After prayer and Scripture reading, any competent person could stand before the congregation to explain the Scriptures. The presiding officer (or president of the synagogue) usually invited visiting teachers to give the exposition or sermon (see

Acts 13:15). In his early ministry Jesus naturally had many chances to speak in the synagogue.

Picture how you might have felt that sabbath day when the guest preacher named Jesus showed up in Capernaum. Perhaps the typical Jew was expecting a warmed-over interpretation gotten from others who were scribes. What a surprise!

Authoritative teaching.—As soon as the sabbath day arrived, Jesus went straight to the synagogue and taught (v. 21). Technically the Jewish sabbath began at sunset on Friday and ended at sunset on Saturday; but Saturday was considered the sabbath day.

The people were dumbfounded at the doctrinal teaching of Jesus because he taught without footnotes. The sermonizing of rabbi-quoting scribes was just the opposite. The scribes' authority was borrowed; Jesus' authority was his own (v. 22). He gave the meaning of God's Word without referring to what "Rabbi So-and-So" said it meant.

Powerful healing.—At this point an unclean spirit came face to face with Jesus and screamed through the lips of the man he possessed (vv. 23–24). If Jesus were speaking today, we don't know how he would describe this man's condition. It is possible that Jesus would say the man was emotionally disturbed or even insane. Such a view is held by some Bible scholars. Other students of the Bible believe that the man was actually demon-possessed. The truth of Jesus' compassionate concern for the hurting continues to show plainly when we accept the first-century diagnosis of demon possession. And that is the position we will continue to examine.

Verse 24 indicates that the man's words belonged to the demon and that the demon spoke for all evil spirits when he said, "What have you to do with us, Jesus of Nazareth?" Translated literally from the Greek text of Mark, this question reads: "What do we have in common?" But in this context, the question has the sense of, "Why do you meddle with us?"

The demon recognized that Jesus had the power to completely ruin all demons and to release their control of people. For that reason, the demonic voice cried out through the man, "Have you come to destroy us? I know who you are, the Holy One of God." The Greek word for "destroy" means complete ruin. It is the same word that is translated "perish" in John 3:16. The evil spirits always sensed Jesus' divine being, and they always cried out when they faced Jesus.

The ordinary Jewish demon-expeller used much magic and many words when he tried to cast out a demon. Jesus simply used an authoritative command: "Be silent, and come out of him!" In verse 25, "Be silent!" is literally, "Be muzzled!" Today we would say, "Hush!"

The unclean spirit left like a storm, with a thunderous shriek and a discharge of power that floored the man (v. 26). All three actions happened at the same time: shaking the man, crying out, and coming out. Luke 4:35 reveals that the demon came out of the man without hurting him.

A stirring response.—"Questioned" (v. 27) shows that the people were puzzled and wondering at the fresh new quality of Jesus' teaching and power. The Jews were familiar with rituals for casting out demons, but they were not familiar with Jesus' single-sentence authority to make demons obey. But all Jesus ever needed to cast out demons was the authority of his spoken word.

Jesus brought the good news; he was the good news; and on that sabbath he made good news. His fame spread faster than a grass fire in a drought.

Private Healing (1:29–31)

Jesus and his four disciples (Andrew, Peter, James, and John) went straight to Peter's house after they left the synagogue. Jesus made Peter's home his headquarters when he was in Galilee (see 2:1; 3:19; 9:33; 10:10).

Obviously, the disciples had already learned to take all their troubles to Jesus, for they immediately told him about the high fever of Peter's mother-in-law (v. 30). The sense of urgency in human need and in Jesus' ability to meet human need is seen in Mark's frequent use of the word "immediately" (vv. 29–30). Mark used the term "immediately" nine times in chapter 1 alone.

Jesus was just as compassionate in private as in public. He instantly healed Peter's mother-in-law by simply coming to her, taking her hand, and lifting her. In the healing of a demoniac, Jesus had spoken a command; but in the healing of a fever-ridden women, Jesus grasped her hand and lifted her up.

The fever left Peter's mother-in-law, and she began to serve Jesus and his disciples (probably by preparing dinner). Her service was a sign of complete cure. When fever leaves a sick person, the person usually remains weak from the fever. But when Jesus healed the hurting, he completely healed them. Both this miracle and the previous one were performed on the sabbath.

Caring for the Crowd (1:32–34)

Healing on the sabbath was considered working on the sabbath; and though no conflict came about over the healings we have just studied, the crowds decided to wait until the end of the sabbath to come to Jesus for healing.

Mark vividly pinpointed what the crowd had waited for: the end of the sabbath. "Evening" (v. 32) might be before or after darkness; so, with more precision, Mark added "at sundown." Sunset ended the sabbath for the Jews. Then people could carry the diseased and the demonized without breaking rabbinic law. The Greek language shows that a steady stream of suffering humanity flooded the door of Peter's house. The Oriental of the Middle East would say "the whole city" and still not mean every last person (v. 33). We make similar statements with similar meanings today.

Jesus cared for the crowd just as he had cared for the individuals. Verse 34 says that Jesus healed "many" who were sick; that terminology was a figure of speech to indicate that he healed all who were brought to him. Matthew 8:16 clearly points out that Jesus healed all who were brought to him.

Jesus habitually let people draw the conclusion that he was the Messiah—the Savior; then he would verify the fact. But he planned for this knowledge to come from his words and works, not from the testimony of a demon or even from persons he had healed at this stage in his ministry. The demons knew the true identity of Jesus, but Jesus would not let them tell it (v. 34).

A Double Pursuit (1:35–39)

Peter and his companions—likely the other disciples—hunted for Jesus. In fact, everyone was searching for Jesus (v. 37). "Followed him" (v. 36) literally meant that they tracked him down.

While people were trying to find Jesus, Jesus was praying for the will of his Father (v. 35). Perhaps Jesus prayed about where to preach. He had the difficult decision of staying with the unending demands of Capernaum or of broadening his ministry. The decision was one of obedience: He extended his ministry throughout all of Galilee (vv.

38–39). Jesus made a habit of getting by himself and praying before he made major decisions, and that habit is a pattern for us.

Curing the Incurable (1:40–42)

For other diseases there was a prescribed rabbinic remedy, but for leprosy there was no cure; yet, Jesus cured the incurable. A hopeful, kneeling leper begged Jesus to heal him (v. 40). No one knows what kind of leprosy the man had because there were several types of leprosy and many other skin diseases that were called leprosy (see Lev. 13—14). Whatever kind of leprosy the man had, it was a kind that made him miserable and an unclean outcast.

Jesus compassionately focused on this person who had a disease worse than death. Leprosy was terminal, but it seemed interminable since it sometimes might last for as long as thirty years. Heartbreaking loneliness accompanied the leper's physical pain and mental anguish. But Jesus didn't want to segregate and isolate the man again; he wanted to give him back his life. So Jesus touched the untouchable and healed him. With the touch of the Master's hand came the words, "I will; be clean" (v. 41); and the cleansing was immediate (v. 42). Jesus cared—and he cares—for the hurting. No one is too sick, too unlovely, or too far gone spiritually to be beyond the concern of Jesus.

Secrecy and Sacrifice (1:43–44)

Jesus sternly charged the healed leper not to tell who had healed him; then Jesus sent the man out (vv. 43–44). Jesus had a purpose in commanding silence, but he did not tell the man the reason for the secrecy.

People did not consider leprosy a sin, but they did think that leprosy was an act of God and that the Messiah would be able to heal leprosy (see Matt. 11:5; Luke 4:27). The Mosaic law prescribed ceremonial cleansing for anyone whose leprosy happened to go away (which was considered a miracle of God's grace). The cleansing Jesus spoke of in Mark 1:44 is detailed in Leviticus 14:1–32.

Disobedience and Hindrance (1:45)

The cleansed leper defiled himself when he disobediently made headline news with his "secret." Hindrance to Jesus' work was the result of disobedience. The unwanted publicity brought such a crowd that Jesus could not openly enter a city.

These passages show that a dominant chord in the life of Jesus was caring for the hurting. He dealt with demons, cooled a fever-racked body, and risked the defilement of touching a leper. It is true that no one ever cared—and still cares—for man like Jesus did. His example makes even the most compassionate disciple seem "care-less" by comparison. We have not begun to tap the harmony and variations of life in Christ if caring for others is not a dominant chord in our lives.

The Beginning of Conflict
2:1 to 3:6

The incidents recorded in Mark 2:1 to 3:6 introduce the element of conflict in response to Jesus' ministry. The relationship between Jesus and other people is an interesting study. Those with crippled bodies and disturbed minds accepted Jesus' revolutionary actions and attitudes because they needed help, and he made them whole. But those who were sick of soul and were least aware of their own needs attacked Jesus for what he did and for what he believed. The conflict challenges readers to examine their own lives and to respond positively to Jesus, the person of good news.

The Setting (2:1 to 3:6)

Jesus returned to Capernaum from preaching in other towns in Galilee. Galilee was the most northern province of Palestine, and it surrounded the western shores of the Sea of Galilee. Jesus called almost all of his disciples in Galilee, and he spent the larger part of his ministry there. Some of the towns in Galilee were Nazareth, Cana, and Capernaum. Capernaum was the headquarters of his Galilean ministry; and while he was there, Jesus made his home with Simon Peter and the other disciples. Capernaum was on the northern shore of the Sea of Galilee. The thriving seaside community was a melting pot of nationalities where beliefs could easily come into conflict. In that setting Jesus performed miracles and taught truths that electrified the air and ruled out a neutral position toward him.

Infirmity and Faith (2:1–5)

Jesus had been back in Capernaum only a short time before people spread the word that he was there. Then the crowds swarmed around Jesus, and he began to preach "the word" (v. 2). Although Mark did not spell out the content of the preaching here, Jesus undoubtedly was preaching good news about God's kingdom and telling about the need for repentance and forgiveness (see Mark 1:14–15). The home probably belonged to Peter and Andrew (see Mark 1:29).

While Jesus was preaching the good news to a packed house that overflowed, four men brought a paralytic for Jesus to heal. (The King James Version reads *palsy*, but that is old English for paralysis; both the Greek text and the context show that the man was unable to walk.) The wall of people and the preaching did not stop the lame man's four friends. They unroofed part of the house and disrupted the preaching service to place the paralytic before Jesus. No wonder Mark said that Jesus *saw* their faith. The lame man seemingly shared the belief of his bed-bearers that Jesus could heal his paralysis. Of course Jesus could heal lame bodies, but in this case he saw a greater need: Jesus saw the need for forgiveness. If Jesus was preaching about repentance and forgiveness, the response came before the invitation at the end of the sermon. So Jesus forgave the man's sins.

We have to read between the lines and read on in the following verses to see that the man's spiritual condition and his physical infirmity were related to each other. In his pronouncement of forgiveness, Jesus took care of both problems at one time. However, what should have been a reason for gladness was an occasion for criticism and conflict.

Belief or Blasphemy (2:6–12)

Jesus' declaration that the man's sins were forgiven shocked the theological minds of the scribes. They knew that only God could forgive sins (vv. 6–7). Therefore, the scribes had only two alternatives: either to believe that Jesus was divine or to accuse him of blasphemy. The scribes silently chose the charge of blasphemy as their first accusation against Jesus (and also as their final accusation—see Mark 14:64). The scribes were the grammatical and editorial nitpickers of their day. Although they were laymen with another occupation to make their living, it was their job to copy the biblical texts, keep them pure, and expound their meaning. We owe a lot to good grammarians and editors, but it is easy to see how these first-century scribes would find it hard to accept change and natural to criticize. Later, the scribes would be joined in their criticism and opposition to Jesus by Pharisees, elders, priests, Sadducees, and Herodians—as well as the fickle crowds and the spineless Roman rulers. But one wonders, *If I had been there, would I have believed Jesus, or would I have accused him of blasphemy?*

Any man could have said, "Your sins are forgiven" (vv. 5,9); but what man could actually have taken away sins and proved that he had done so? No one but Jesus! In the question of verse 9, the pronouncement of forgiveness and the command to arise were equally within Jesus' province. However, only the command to arise could give visible proof of the forgiveness; so Jesus told the paralytic to get up and to carry his bed home (vv. 11–12).

Jesus, God-man, had brought the forgiveness of God to man, and all of the people there—apparently even the scribes—admitted that they had never seen anything like it before (v. 12). And the people praised God.

Mark is the shortest of the four Gospels, and it collects and compresses many events. So Mark did not go into all the details related to the lame man's forgiveness and healing. But it is worth noting that repentance and faith are requirements for forgiveness. The change of heart and mind that turns to Jesus in trust must have taken place in the heart of the lame man just as it must take place in our hearts if God through Christ is to make us whole. There were others— then and now—who needed to surrender to Jesus.

Sudden Surrender (2:13–14)

From conflict and resolution, Jesus went to the seaside and taught as he walked with the ever-present crowd. Then Jesus came upon a tax collector. Capernaum was a customs center where Levi (commonly known as Matthew) worked at the job of collecting taxes.

Levi was an unlikely prospect for discipleship since he bore the stigma of having sold out to Rome. He collected taxes for a foreign people who occupied the country, and he also lived off those taxes. But, as Jesus always does, he saw unrealized potential in Levi; and he called him to discipleship. That call meant that Jesus wanted Levi to follow him, to learn from him, to obey him, and to lead others to do the same. Levi responded with a once-and-for-all commitment that cost him his job, but it was the best decision of his life. Beyond Levi's sudden surrender to discipleship and the radical change it brought about in his life, we don't know very much about Levi. We do know that the nature of his call and response was more important than his name and history.

Tragedy and Triviality (2:15–17)

Pharisees were religious leaders among the Jews who dedicated their whole lives to the study and teaching of the Law. The Pharisees shared many of the beliefs that Jesus held, but they seemingly could not separate what was important from what was unimportant in matters of religion. We see that fact illustrated here.

The Pharisees avoided the common people who did not keep the ceremonial law of man-made interpretations and were, therefore, counted "sinners." Further, the Pharisees despised the greedy Jewish publicans (tax collectors) who mingled with the Gentiles (anyone who was not Jewish) and practiced dishonesty for a living. But Jesus gladly attended a dinner that may have been Levi's plan to introduce other "sinners" and tax collectors to Jesus.

The smug scribes and Pharisees would not have kept company with Levi and his kind of people; so, with resentment and pettiness, they implied that Jesus was wrong to associate with people who had need in their lives. It was tragic that the self-righteous leaders saw no need for Jesus in their own lives; that failure kept them from being helped by the Great Physician. The accusation against Jesus was trivial, but what it revealed about the scribes and Pharisees was tragic. And there would be more of the same kind of thing about traditions and the sabbath.

Time and Tradition (2:18–22)

The disciples of John and the disciples of the Pharisees were fasting, and they wanted to know why Jesus' nonconforming disciples were out of step with tradition (see Matt. 9:14; Luke 5:33). Those who followed John the Baptist and those who followed the way of the Pharisees may have fasted for different reasons, but fasting was a part of the religious observance of both groups. However, the Old Testament commanded fasting only once a year: on the Day of Atonement (Ex. 20:10; Lev. 16:1–34; 23:26–32; 25:9; Num. 29:9–11). By the New Testament era, Pharisees were fasting regularly on Mondays and Thursdays and seemingly making quite a show of it. Fasting could accompany repentance, or it could serve as a sign of mourning. Except for the Day of Atonement, though, fasting was a matter of choice that had become a tradition.

Jesus' answer was perfect. He explained that fasting was an expression and action natural for a funeral, but it was completely out of place at a wedding. He pictured himself as the bridegroom and his disciples as the wedding guests. The principle he made was that circumstances should dictate the time of fasting and that actions should match feelings (v. 20). Verse 20 also indicates that Jesus already felt the shadow of death approaching.

Verses 21–22 contain two brief parables. Jesus used the parables to say that time had run out in the old covenant and that the external forms of Judaism could not contain the radical newness of Christian action. The unshrunk cloth of the new covenant could not be patched onto the worn-out garment of Judaism (v. 21). Likewise, the covenant wine could not be kept in the rigid, old wineskin of Judaism. Fresh wine should be put in unused wineskins, which were flexible enough to expand without bursting. Jesus knew that his message called for dramatic change and that only those who were flexible enough to receive new truth could make the transition. Tradition has its place, but it also has its time; and when the time is up, it is the right thing to change and move forward under God's guidance.

Precedent and Priority (2:23–28)

According to the Pharisees, the disciples of Jesus were guilty of working on the sabbath. The disciples had pulled some grain, husked it between their hands, and eaten it (vv. 23–24). This practice would have been all right in the eyes of the Pharisees on any other day of the week. The accusation was not theft but a charge of working on the sabbath (see Deut. 23:25).

Time and again the religious leaders accused Jesus of breaking the sabbath. The Pharisees had gotten things reversed; they had forgotten that the sabbath was made for man and not man for the sabbath. They and their ancestors had set up a burdensome and unneeded mess of rules to ensure the proper keeping of the sabbath. Jesus observed the sabbath as God intended for it to be kept and not as man had misunderstood for it to be kept.

In this case, Jesus did not deny the charge of the Pharisees, but he defended the behavior of his disciples with a precedent from the life of David (see Mark 2:25–26; 1 Sam. 21:1–6). The Pharisees faced the dilemma of having to condemn David if they condemned the disciples. David had also broken the ceremonial law when it became necessary. So the precedent introduced the principle of verse 27: Man's emergency needs have priority over the sabbath law of complete rest. Jesus actually restored the sabbath to its original place of serving man rather than enslaving him. Verse 28 means that Jesus had authority over the sabbath. The Pharisees never understood or accepted this truth.

In fact, the Pharisees failed to understand and accept Jesus' self-revelation. In verse 10 he had referred to himself as the "Son of man" who had authority to forgive sins. In verses 19–20 he had referred to himself as the bridegroom who obviously was ushering in a new era. In verse 28 he referred to himself as the "Son of man" who was master of the sabbath. Jesus used these self-designations to refer to himself as the Messiah. But as the next sabbath scene shows, the Pharisees remained blind to who he was.

Religious Rigor Mortis (3:1–6)

Jesus had a habit of healing on the sabbath, and the religious leaders made a habit of condemning him for it (vv. 1–2). Jesus' critics were never those who had physical needs; they were always those who unknowingly had spiritual needs. Jesus was thinking about giving a man's life back to him, and the Pharisees were thinking about accusing and killing (vv. 2,6).

Jesus knew that the Pharisees intended to condemn him for healing on the sabbath, so he questioned them about the law of the sabbath: Was it right to help and save, or to hurt and kill? The Pharisees condemned themselves with silence as much as if they had answered, "Yes, it was right to help and save," and then had condemned Jesus for doing what they had admitted was right. Their rigid hearts and spiritual blindness brought Jesus momentary anger but permanent grief, for the Pharisees had rejected him (v. 5).

Jesus spoke the healing words to the man who had a need, and the man was healed. Immediately, the Pharisees exploded and stalked out to the Roman-catering Herodians (who were the Pharisees' natural enemies) to plot the death of Jesus.

In looking at these conflicts over the sabbath, Mark seemingly collected incidents over several sabbaths. The abuse of the sabbath in that day was a narrow legalism. Although the New Testament era saw the day of worship and rest change from Saturday to Sunday, the idea of one special day each week for worship and rest continued. And in our era the abuse has changed from a narrow legalism to an anything-goes attitude.

Many people have used passages like these in Mark to justify work or anything else they want to do on the Lord's Day. People glibly say as an excuse for failing to observe a day of worship, "The ox was in the ditch" (see Luke 14:5 for the origin and context). But as others have said when this excuse becomes routine, "Either fill in the ditch, or kill the ox." Jesus set the example for behavior on the sabbath; he did not lessen or do away with the day of worship, but he did clarify its purpose.

Ministering and Being Misunderstood
3:7–35

Jesus continued his Galilean ministry, but that ministry entered a new phase: a changed location, a more varied congregation, and a call to twelve special disciples. Between recent conflict and approaching misunderstanding, Jesus went to the sea and then to a mountain.

A Seaside Retreat (3:7–12)

Jesus and his disciples retreated to the seaside. Was the retreat because of the plot to kill Jesus, or was it for spiritual refreshment? The Bible doesn't say, but perhaps both elements were present. It was not time for Jesus to die; it was time for him to continue his ministry. So he moved his ministry from the closed-in synagogue to the wide-open amphitheater of the seaside. He had ministered mostly to the Galilean Jews, but now Jews and Gentiles alike swarmed in from every direction because they had heard the incredible stories about Jesus and his healing power. The conflicts had not hurt Jesus' popularity with those who recognized their need for his help. Though the unwieldy crowd knew little of the motive and mission of Jesus, they sensed that he really could heal their diseases and make them whole.

The sick people literally threw themselves against Jesus in their belief that mere contact would bring a cure (v. 10). Jesus did not mind touching or being touched by the untouchables (see Mark 1:40–41); but the crowd was about to crush him. So Jesus told his disciples to keep a boat ready in case he needed to move out into the water.

Perhaps the unclean spirits were the only ones who really understood who Jesus was, but Jesus ordered them not to speak (vv. 11–12). The unfolding drama of Jesus' messiahship was on a timetable that called for Jesus to reveal who he was—in his own way and in his own time. He would not use the unclean spirits who were disciples of Satan; rather, he would choose his own disciples to witness about him and about the nature of his discipleship.

A Mountaintop Experience (3:13–19*a*)

From the seaside, Jesus went to a mountaintop experience. Out of the multitude Jesus selected a choice group to gather before him on the hillside (v. 13). And from that group Jesus formally appointed the twelve who would serve as his disciples and apostles. The appointment and training of the twelve was one of the most important aspects of the entire ministry of Jesus. After the death and resurrection of Jesus, the commitment and the ability of the twelve would be crucial to the continued spread of the good news. So it is important to understand what Jesus called the twelve to be and to do.

The twelve were to be disciples.—Disciple means a learner, a pupil, an apprentice. Jesus called the disciples to be with him: to learn his ways, his teachings, his attitudes, and his applications of truth. They were to stay with Jesus until they moved beyond the apprentice stage. *Disciple* was the favorite word for the twelve in the Gospels. In fact, the word appears only in the Gospels and in Acts. And in Acts the word usually refers to new converts in the general sense of *Christian.*

*The twelve were to be apostles.—*The word *apostle* appears only once in Mark (6:30); but outside of the Gospels, *apostle* was the favorite word in the rest of the New Testament to refer to the twelve. Why? Because *apostle* means one sent on a mission. The Greek language has two words for send; one is a general word that refers to any kind of sending, and the other is a specific word that carries the sense of messenger, ambassador, or missionary. *Apostle* is that specific word. The twelve would go out to preach the good news (see Mark 1:14,38; 2:4), and they would have power to cast out demons (compare 3:15 with 6:12–13). So, broadly speaking, *disciple* refers to staying with Jesus and learning; and *apostle* refers to going and ministering. The transition was natural.

Simon Peter is listed first, and Judas Iscariot is listed last. The beginning and the end are the same in each listing of the disciples except for Acts, when Judas Iscariot was already dead. The lists vary in the sequence of other names (see Matt. 10:2–4; Mark 3:14–19; Luke 6:13–16; and Acts 1:13).

Jesus saw potential in these men. For example, he gave Simon the nickname Peter, which meant rock. Not all of the disciples became what Jesus intended; nevertheless, the potential was there. And the potential for discipleship par excellence lies in each of us.

Mistaken Concern (3:19*b*–21)

Jesus returned home to eat and to rest (perhaps in Simon Peter's home). But the clamoring crowd was insensitive to Jesus' own personal needs, for they had an insatiable appetite of their own: namely, to be with Jesus.

To add to the confusion, well-meaning family members had decided to come and get Jesus because they thought he was out of his head (v. 21). (The group may have included friends other than Jesus' own family; see the King James Version.) Was it not true that Jesus had left the security of home, ignored the safety of religious conformity, and disregarded the verdict of society in choosing his disciples? Jesus took risks that relatives and friends might think were unsensible. Besides all of that, he was not getting the food and rest he needed.

The great truth of Jesus' ministry was so far beyond the understanding of Jesus' family and friends that they wrongly felt he needed to be rescued from himself. This mistaken concern was to lead to a teaching opportunity later (see 3:31-35).

Ridiculous Ridicule (3:22–27)

The law experts from Jerusalem thought that weaker demons could be expelled only by stronger demons; consequently, they accused Jesus of getting his power from the prince of demons, Beelzebul (another name for Satan). The idea was not so much that Jesus had Beelze-

bul as it was that Beelzebul had Jesus. (*Demons* is the correct translation, not *devils;* compare the RSV and KJV. Properly speaking, there
is one devil; but there are many demons.)

The contemptible charge of the scribes loses much of its abrupt-
ness—though none of its absurdity—when we realize that Jesus had
just healed a sightless and voiceless demoniac (Matt. 12:22–24). At
best, the scribes were guilty of misjudgment; at worst, they were
guilty of consciously denying the Holy Spirit as the source of Jesus'
power.

Jesus answered the charge by questioning whether Satan would
cast out Satan; then, without a pause, he answered his own question
with two comparisons. Satan and his demons were members of the
same kingdom (see Matt. 12:26); therefore, they shared the same motivation (see Mark 3:24). Consequently, the power that expelled demons
had to have a moral quality different from that of demons. Further-
more, for a stronger evil spirit to cast out a weaker evil spirit would
be civil war in the evil kingdom. The same would be true of Satan's
household (v. 25). The only logical conclusion was to admit that Satan
could not be the source of Jesus' power, for that would be satanic
suicide (v. 26).

After Jesus had put down the calculated misjudgment of the scribes,
he gave another comparison that showed what had really happened
when he expelled evil spirits (v. 27). Jesus pictured himself as one
stronger than the strong man (Satan). In actuality, Jesus had overpow-
ered Satan and taken control. The truth was apparent: Jesus had divine
power, not satanic power. But those who are spiritually blind cannot
see truth that is apparent.

Permanent Sin (3:28–30)

Blasphemy against the Holy Spirit is a unique sin: It is the only
sinful condition for which there is no possibility of forgiveness. God
gladly forgives every sin when there is actual repentance (see 1 John
1:9). But people who blaspheme the Holy Spirit reveal a spiritual
condition that is incapable of the one condition of forgiveness: that
is, repentance. The consensus of biblical scholarship seems to agree
that the stated sin of blasphemy is an enduring condition, not a temporary act of sin. In a manner of speaking, when the optic nerve of
the soul becomes severed, a person lacks moral discernment; and
he may judge that holy acts come from an unholy spirit rather than

from the Holy Spirit of God. This judgment is the ultimate in misunderstanding.

Only those who have never come to know Jesus as Lord and Savior are capable of the type of blasphemy that has been called the unpardonable sin: namely, slander of the Holy Spirit. And commentators have wisely suggested that fear of having committed the unpardonable sin is the best assurance one can have that he is not yet guilty. Coming to know the saving grace of God through Jesus Christ is the only way to be assured of never committing the unpardonable sin.

Proof of Spiritual Kinship (3:31–35)

The family of Jesus arrived. They were baffled, mistaken, and misunderstanding in their concern; and they planned to take Jesus home (see v. 21). Unbelieving brothers (see John 7:5) and a loving but mistaken mother of Jesus presented a pathetic problem. In all kindness, Jesus used the warm, sacred symbols of brother, sister, and mother to tell all of the world that spiritual kinship is stronger than biological kinship. Those who share Jesus' compulsion to do the will of God are the spiritual kindred of Jesus. But the obedience does not earn the kinship; it only proves it.

Jesus knew from Scripture that commitment to God had to have priority if there came a time when one had to choose between God and family (see Ex. 32:25–29; Deut. 33:8–9). His call to discipleship sometimes involved leaving homes and families (Mark 10:28–30). And in this instance, Jesus' own family had a right motive but a wrong purpose that would interfere with God's will. So Jesus did not respond to the pleas of his family.

It was ironic that friends, critics, and family could look upon the world's only perfectly ordered mind—the mind of Jesus—and judge that mind to be out of order. But that's what happened. Jesus set the example for us by responding to misunderstanding and criticism with patient reasoning. And when patient reasoning did not satisfy his critics, Jesus did not quit his mission or become bitter toward others. He continued to follow the will of God.

The Kingdom of God in Parables
4:1–34

Mark 4:1–34 records a time between two storms: one, an emotional storm of being misunderstood; the other, a literal storm on the Sea of Galilee. But just as dramatic as any storm was the change of Jesus' teaching method. He turned from plain, straightforward teaching to teaching by parables. Jesus had taught by comparison in isolated instances (such as Mark 3:23), but at this stage he turned to parables as his standard method for teaching the crowds. The parables of Mark 4 help us to understand something about the nature of the kingdom of God.

Jesus taught many things by parable, but in this chapter he focused on the kingdom of God. Most scholars believe that Jesus used parables to reveal truth, but there are some perplexing verses in Mark 4 that leave us puzzled about whether Jesus also used parables to conceal truth. Before we examine the parables themselves, we need further insight into "the kingdom of God" and into the purpose of parables; so we will look at five verses that lay a foundation for study of the parables.

Kingdom Comparisons (4:1–2,10–12)

The kingdom of God.—Literally, this term means the reign of God, but the exact and full meaning is as slippery to grasp as quicksilver. The Bible actually defines the kingdom for us in Matthew 6:10. The Hebrews had a way of saying something and then repeating the same idea with different words (known as Hebrew parallelism). We see that form used in Matthew 6:10 to shed light on the meaning of the kingdom of God:

Thy   kingdom   come,
↕   ↕   ↕
Thy   will   be done.

Whether we look upon the kingdom of God as past, present, or future, the primary focus is to be upon the fact that God is doing the ruling. This fact served as the great central truth of Jesus' ministry.

The terms "kingdom of God" and "kingdom of heaven" appear over one hundred times in the Gospels.

The Jewish people were familiar with the term "kingdom of God," but they were not familiar with what it meant to Jesus. They tended to emphasize "kingdom" more than "of God." The Jewish people were under Roman domination, and they wanted the kingdom of God to come now and end the Roman rule; they wanted a victorious Messiah who would rule from a throne. Jesus wanted to rule in man's heart, not on an earthly throne. He wanted his hearers to know these truths about the kingdom of God: (1) It involves the eternal rule of God. (2) It is visible upon earth when those who follow God's will live it out in daily commitment. (3) It will eventually be completed, which is the blessed hope of Christians. To communicate these great truths, Jesus chose parables.

The purpose of parables.—Parables were simple stories from everyday life that shed light on profound spiritual truths. The parables helped make abstract teachings concrete and meaningful—moving from the known to the unknown. Parables left men and women wondering and thinking for themselves rather than dismissing and forgetting truths that were beyond their understanding.

For those who refused to become disciples, Jesus' parables remained riddles (v. 11). If the parables were earthly stories with heavenly meanings, the people understood only the earthly side; the heavenly side remained a mystery to them. Even Jesus' own disciples asked him about the parables, wondering why he used them (see Matt. 13:10). The answer about Jesus' use of parables comes from the context of Mark 4. Jesus used parables for the purpose of teaching (vv. 1–2); so, whatever verse 12 means, it does not mean that Jesus used parables to hide what he was teaching (also, see Mark 4:34). If verse 12 were taken very literally, it would seem to say that Jesus used parables to prevent understanding. Admittedly, some scholars accept that interpretation of the verse; but most scholars do not: They interpret the verse in light of the rest of the Bible. Verse 12 is a partial quotation from Isaiah 6:9–10:

"And he said, 'Go, and say to this people:
  "Hear and hear, but do not understand;
  see and see, but do not perceive."
  Make the heart of this people fat,
    and their ears heavy,
    and shut their eyes;

> lest they see with their eyes,
>> and hear with their ears,
> and understand with their hearts,
>> and turn and be healed.'"

Because of the Isaiah background, Mark 4:12 seems to be a proverb that shows the spiritual blindness and deafness of those who choose not to let God rule their lives.

With this introduction to the kingdom of God and the purpose of parables, we are prepared to study the parables themselves. Jesus had returned to the seashore and used a boat as his pulpit (see Mark 3:9). He spoke his parables to the multitudes; then he patiently explained the full meaning privately to his disciples (also see Mark 4:33–34). The kingdom of God was no longer a mystery to the disciples; it was a secret that they were in on (compare the KJV with the RSV). In the New Testament, "mystery" referred to what had been hidden but was now revealed to disciples. But the disciples still needed a lot of teaching, and Jesus provided that. Now let us look at a parable that Jesus told twice.

Kingdom Responses (4:3–9,13–20)

Unlike most parables, the parable of the sower has more than one main point: The double thrust comes from both the condition of the soil and the yield from the seed.

The parable of the sower tells about the growth of the kingdom and the conditions for that growth. The uniformly good seed refers to the good news of the kingdom, while the soil of varying conditions refers to those who hear the good news.

In Palestine the planters first scattered their seed; then they plowed the ground. No wonder Jesus' hearers could picture every detail of the story. From everyday life they knew the farmer could never know his proportion of yield until he knew the condition of the soil.

In the story there are four kinds of soil: (1) wayside soil that served as a path and was beaten down so that it was like cement, (2) a thin layer of surface soil that was bedded on limestone, (3) soil that was polluted by thorns, and (4) soil that was pure, rich, and deep. Jesus told the parable in verses 3–9 without interpreting its spiritual meaning. Basically, the meaning was this: Get the soil of your life in shape so that you can receive the seed of the good news and then bear spiritual fruit as God reigns in your life (see v. 9). However, Jesus interpreted the spiritual meaning in verses 13–19 after his disciples asked him for an explanation. The conditions of the four soils are matched by four types of conditions in the lives of those who hear the good news.

Cementlike hearers do not receive the word at all; it just goes in one ear and out the other. Hearers in this group may be preoccupied or self-righteous. Whatever the reason for not receiving the word, Satan takes the word away before it germinates.

Surface-soil hearers immediately and gladly receive the word and show signs of promise, but they respond before counting the cost of discipleship. The seed that germinates first then withers with the sun of hardship because it lacks roots. An old church building was leveled and the basement filled in with rock so that there was no evidence of what lay under the thin coat of soil. Each spring the first grass to green was that over the site of the old church building; it appeared as a rectangle. The grass within that rectangle withered and died with the heat of summer because its roots could not get through the rock. The other grass greened later, but it endured when the heat came. The lives of many hearers reflect a similar condition.

Polluted-soil hearers are those who hear the word and take it in, but it fails to bear fruit in their lives. Just as thorns and weeds can choke a garden, the thorny cares of life can keep the good news from bearing fruit in a life. Some people give first-rate loyalty to secondary things; they are double-minded. Their priorities get out of order, and God's word gets choked out by inferior concerns.

But *good-soil hearers* receive the word and bear a large amount of fruit. This kind of soil is rich, pure, and beautiful. It is represented in the lives of those who serve God wholeheartedly and single-mindedly. Farmers in the day of Jesus' parable counted ten stems per seed a good harvest, but forty or more would be counted a bumper crop. Good-soil hearers bear that kind of crop.

The tragedy was that only one of the four types of soil produced any lasting results. Three types of soil received the seed in vain. Man is like the nonproductive soils when the soil of his soul is not prepared to receive the seed of the kingdom—the reign of God. The fertilizer business is based on the fact that soil can be changed. Through complete surrender to God's grace, the hard soil can become soft; the shallow soil can become deep; the thorny soil can become pure; and each of us can belong to the good-soil group.

Some scholars believe the parable teaches only that the condition of the soil determines whether the gospel will have any effect. Others have concluded that the parable teaches that the kingdom of God will overcome all barriers to increase the reign of God. Finally, and logically, most scholars have suggested that Jesus intended both emphases: the importance of attentive and responsive hearers along with the inevitable, abundant growth of the kingdom of God.

Kingdom Responsibilities (4:21–25)

A saucer-type lamp containing oil and a wick was essential for every home in the time of Jesus' earthly ministry; consequently, Jesus would have expected a smile and a silent no to his question: "Is a lamp brought in to be put under a bushel, or under a bed, and not on a stand?" (v. 21). A bushel would hide the light, and a bed (really, a pad on the floor in those days) would smother it. A lamp was used only to give light. (Note that in the KJV "manifested" means visible— v. 22.)

The parable of the lamp shows the responsibility that comes with kingdom citizenship. Each Christian is like a lamp, lighted for the one purpose of illuminating the good news. And the good news is that God will give eternal life when an individual lets God reign in his heart. Some scholars think that verse 22 means the disciples were to keep the secret of the kingdom until the ascension of Christ. And it is true that premature revelations confuse and bewilder minds not ready to receive them. But, all in all, verse 22 seems to teach that the ultimate purpose of parables is to heighten and illuminate truth rather than conceal it.

Verses 24–25 express the law of nature: We either use what we have or lose it. This law is true of the spiritual realm as well as the physical. Growth comes with usage; atrophy comes with lack of usage. (Matt. 25:14–30 could serve as a commentary on these verses. That passage deals with talents and describes wickedness as the sin of doing nothing with what you have.)

In summary, verses 21–25 teach that truth is meant to be revealed (vv. 21–22), that learning requires hearing and obedient action (v. 23), and that a person's getting is determined by his giving (vv. 24–25).

Kingdom Certainty (4:26–29)

We can almost sense the feeling of futility that plagued the disciples of Jesus. What little they had seen of the kingdom of God was disappointingly meager. But this parable, which is unique to Mark, tells about the seed growing by itself; and it has been called the parable to end discouragement.

The secret and the certainty of the kingdom's growth is in the nature of the sown seed and its interaction with the right type of soil. When seed and soil get together, God assures growth of the kingdom. Man can become aware of the growth and appreciate it even though he doesn't understand it.

Although God is the power behind kingdom growth, this parable makes three demands upon those who labor with God: faithful sowing of the seed, patient waiting, and joyful reaping. Man has a part in kingdom growth, but God has the power. The certainty is that a time is coming when all the world will recognize that God is King and will submit to his reign. No power can hinder that certainty; and with that truth in mind, we can be certain that the kingdom grows irresistibly.

This parable of patience shows us that although the kingdom's growth may be unnoticeable, we can be assured that its growth is constant, unfailing, and moving toward its completion. With such assurance, we are called to plant the seed of God's word and leave the growth of it with him. Then, when the harvest is ripe, we must reap it. The thought contains a challenge to be bold in the mission of spreading God's kingdom.

Kingdom Completion (4:30–32)

The mustard seed is about the size of a pinhead, but proverbially it stood for the smallest thing possible. (The cypress seed and other seeds were smaller.) In Palestine the mustard mushroomed from a tiny seed to a shrub eight to twelve feet high, and birds settled on the shrub to pick the black seeds out of the pod.

The power of the comparison lay in the great ending that came from the small beginning. The mind of the Hebrews could appreciate this comparison, for the Hebrews tended to see the beginning and the end—not the process. Comparing the beginning and the end makes growth measurable and visible. In an age that wants instant everything, Jesus' parable is a reminder that great things take time. And God honors small beginnings and the cultivation of those efforts on a day-by-day basis.

Without making each detail of the parable mean something that was not intended, still we need to comment on the tree and on the birds. "Birds of the air" was a phrase used by the rabbis to mean all people, including the Gentiles (non-Jews). Then, in the Old Testament, a tree and its branches often stood for a great empire. So the picture of completion seems built into this parable of growth.

There are scholars who argue for interpretations other than the one you just read, but the interpretation given seems in keeping with the optimism of the chapter as it tells of the kingdom of God. Further, the New Testament emphasizes that the kingdom of God will come to a point of grand completion.

We always need to remember that the kingdom of God has to do with God's rule. While time exists, God lets individuals choose to accept or reject his rule—though he remains in charge of everything. While time continues, the kingdom may look as small as a mustard seed in relationship to the multitudes who refuse to accept God's kingly rule. But when time ends and the kingdom is complete, not one person will deny the complete rule and authority of God. But even now the kingdom has grown greatly from its small beginnings.

Parable Epilogue (4:33–34)

Jesus told other parables to the crowd as long as they were able to understand them. ("Hear" obviously included understanding.) Verse 33 confirms the fact that Jesus used the parables as teaching tools and not as a means to hide knowledge from people. Nevertheless, Jesus customarily gave the disciples fuller explanation of the parables when the crowds had gone (v. 34). In fact, the discerning reader can see that Jesus began a more intensive teaching of the disciples who were to carry on his kingdom work after he ascended to heaven. The parables were memorable stories for everyone, but the close circle of Jesus' disciples had the benefit of detailed interpretation to go along with the vivid illustration from daily life.

Kingdom Summary (4:1–34)

Over and over again the term "kingdom" has demanded our attention. The concept of the kingdom of God is too great for us to understand in its fullness. Perhaps this greatness is exactly why Jesus chose to use parables: to compare the kingdom to things that were easy to understand instead of trying to give a definition.

Though there continues to be a mystery about the kingdom, Jesus' main teachings stand out: (1) The kingdom of God is the rule of God. (2) The productive spiritual life is the one that gladly submits to God's rule. (3) Each Christian has a responsibility to let God use him in the bearing of spiritual fruit for the growth of the kingdom. (4) Witnessing Christians are responsible for faithfulness, not for quantity of results. However, the results are often invisible or imperceptible to our eyes. (5) God can change a person just as types of soil can change. (6) The kingdom of God is both present and future, but personal decisions in the present will show up in many ways in the future when the kingdom is completed. (7) The kingdom of God grows and moves toward completion through those who faithfully share the good news with others.

Jesus' Power in Action
4:35 to 6:6

The parables taught about the reign of God. Now we enter a new part of Jesus' ministry that shows God's reign in action. Through four miracles, Jesus ruled over nature, demons, disease, and death—but not over unbelief. His display of power would serve as further preparation for the future ministry of the disciples. To perform their ministry, they also would need the power that comes from God, a power like that which Jesus had.

Power Over Nature (4:35–41)

Jesus had taught from a boat until evening came. Then, at Jesus' suggestion, the disciples joined him in the boat to go across the sea from Capernaum to Gadara. The trip from the northwestern shore to the eastern shore of the Sea of Galilee was about six miles. Mark is the only Gospel that tells about other boats accompanying them (vv. 35–36).

More often than not, the Sea of Galilee was calm and peaceful; yet it was notorious for its sudden storms. Jesus' disciples had set sail calmly enough with Jesus asleep on a cushion (at the rear of the boat, where a guest would lie down). But a violent storm erupted, and waves began to fill the boat. The disciples were seasoned fisher-men who would not panic over a few whitecaps. But the boat was almost swamped and was in danger of sinking; so they were panic-stricken. Jesus must have been exhausted from the strain of teaching, for he was sleeping through the storm. Although his sleep was one of weariness, it was also one of faith; he had no fear. With mingled agitation and reproach, the disciples woke Jesus and questioned whether it mattered to him that they were about to drown. (These same disciples would later sleep when Jesus needed them.)

Jesus quickly calmed the disciples' alarm with a command to the elements. The creator of the wind and sea commanded them, "Peace! Be still!" (v. 39). And the storm disappeared. For the first time in the book of Mark, Jesus revealed that he had power over the elements of nature. And, as some commentators point out, if you accept a heal-ing miracle, why stagger at a nature miracle? The Creator is also lord over his creation. As the King James Version states it, "There arose a great storm of wind, . . . and he arose" (vv. 37,39). Truly, for every crisis there is Christ.

After Jesus calmed the storm, he questioned the disciples about their fear and lack of faith. "Afraid" (v. 40) may also mean cowardly (as *The New English Bible* translates it). In Jesus' gentle rebuke of the disciples, he revealed that faith is the cure for fear (v. 40). Then when fear seized the disciples again, Jesus did not chide them; the second fear was the awe that man should have—a reverent fear at the power of God in Jesus (v. 41). No command in the Bible appears more often than "Fear not!" Faith in Jesus ends cowardly fear. But the modern Christian needs a healthy and wholesome fear of Jesus, which causes the Christian to stand in awe and to wonder at the personhood of one who has such great power.

Some scholars try to explain away the miracle over the elements of nature. But the God who created the world did not create it to be a closed system, sealed off from him. He can—and does—intervene in his creation. In the calming of the wind and sea, God in Christ overruled the disorder of nature.

Power Over Demons (5:1–20)

When Jesus got off the boat at Gadara (the country of the Gerasenes), he met a demoniac of the worst order. Today some people would say the man was demon-possessed; others would say he was mentally ill. Educated, well-trained, emotionally stable missionaries tell of having seen evidences of demon possession. They have seen the power and the darkness of evil and have testified that they could see no other explanation than demon possession. In civilized societies, others have spoken of witnessing demon possession. And it is no secret that many people worship Satan. Other intelligent Christians, who also try to interpret the Bible accurately, believe that demon possession refers to mental illness. The Bible often speaks of demons as literal beings and offers no apology or detailed explanation. And Jesus treated the demons as the Bible refers to them.

Whatever term you may use, the fact is that Jesus met a situation where opposition to God's will had gotten the upper hand in a man's life. The man was as storm-tossed by the demons as the disciples had been by the storm in nature. Running wild with superhuman strength, night and day, the man disturbed others and tortured himself (vv. 2–5). The demoniac is said to have worshiped Jesus (RSV), but *worship* probably should be translated "knelt before" (v. 6). With a loud shriek, the demon-possessed man called the divine name of Jesus and asked what he wanted. Then, with an oath that used the name of God, the demons within the man begged Jesus not to torment them by casting them out (vv. 7–8).

When Jesus asked the demoniac his name, the demons answered through the man that their name was "Legion" for there were many of them (v. 9). A legion was a Roman army unit of from forty-five hundred to six thousand men, but the term could simply refer to a large number. (In the New Testament, legion refers only to armies of demons or hosts of angels.) In verses 9–13 notice the intermingling of singular and plural pronouns. The one man was possessed by many demons. They had taken over the man's life to the extent that he scarcely reflected anything of the image of God, but he had the potential of being conformed to the image of Jesus (see Rom. 8:29).

Since the demons knew they would be expelled from the man and from the country, they begged Jesus to let them inhabit the two thousand hogs that were nearby (v. 12). Jesus granted the request. Whatever the number of demons—two thousand, six thousand, or some other number—there were more than enough to drive the hogs crazy and into the sea, where they drowned. The destructive purpose of the demons was indicated by the destruction of the hogs (v. 13).

Jesus' power changed a naked, insane cemetery dweller into a clothed, coherent man who could go home. The reaction of the people was mixed. The herdsmen undoubtedly moaned over their loss. Others were so shocked and afraid when they heard what happened that they begged Jesus to leave. Only one man wanted to follow Jesus; he was the man Jesus healed. "Be with him" (v. 18) seems to have been a technical term for discipleship in Mark (see 3:14). In other words, the grateful witness wanted to become Jesus' disciple and follow him. But, in effect, Jesus said, "You follow me by staying home and telling what I have done for you" (v. 19). Jesus did not put any restriction on the man as he had in other cases of healing. Perhaps it was because the man was in a Gentile land, and Jesus would be leaving to go back among the Jews.

The man obeyed Jesus! Throughout the ten Greek cities known as the Decapolis, he announced the powerful, compassionate thing Jesus had done for him (v. 20). The people were amazed at the healed man's testimony.

People often wonder about the hogs. They were forbidden meat to the Jews (see Lev. 11:7). But it was natural for the Gentiles to have hogs. Although pockets of Jews lived in the Decapolis, the ten cities were primarily made up of Gentiles. The important thing was not the ownership or death of the hogs; it was the new life and image Jesus gave when he freed a man from the demonic.

Power Over Disease (5:21–34)

Jesus once more crossed the sea and met a crowd. This time the crowd included a synagogue ruler (or administrator) named Jairus. Jairus' little daughter lay near death. So he forgot both his personal pride and the dignity of his office as he fell at Jesus' feet and begged Jesus to come and heal his daughter. Jairus' request was urgent, and Jesus' response was immediate: He started to Jairus' home. The crowd followed (vv. 21–24).

On the way to Jairus' home, a woman who had suffered with a disease for twelve long years silently pushed through the crowd, hoping to steal a miracle from Jesus. Her condition was desperate. She was poor, weak, ceremonially unclean (Lev. 15:25–27), friendless, unknown, and continually suffering from an embarrassing condition. She had bled for as many years as Jairus' daughter was old. During those years, she had spent all her money on doctors; but instead of being better, her condition was worse. (Luke the physician recorded that the doctors were not able to make her better, but he did not say that the woman's condition worsened—see Luke 8:43.) Undoubtedly, the woman had tried all of the eleven cures prescribed in the Talmud (a book of Jewish writings). But for all her trouble, she was not better, but worse. Yet, in her helplessness, she had not become hopeless. Jesus was her last resort. Over and over again she had told herself that she would be healed if she could just touch the hem of Jesus' garment. So, secretly and from behind, she touched the hem of Jesus' garment with the faith that she would be healed. Instantly, after twelve years of misery, she was healed.

Jesus' healing always took something out of him. He immediately felt the cost of that healing. When Jesus asked who had touched him, he was asking who had been healed. The cleansed woman had risked contaminating Jesus ceremonially with her touch, so with fear and trembling she confessed what she had done. Jesus did not condemn her; rather, he commended her faith, ordered her the blessing of peace, and assured her that her healing was complete. No one is so contaminated with disease or sin that he can't approach Jesus for his healing touch.

When Jesus spoke to the healed woman, he called her *daughter* (v. 34). This incident was the only time that Jesus ever addressed a woman with that term. She had proved that she was a child of faith. And Jesus had proved once again that he had power over disease.

Power Over Death (5:35–43)

How Jairus, the anxious father, had endured the seemingly long interruption we do not know. The woman had been able to endure the disease for twelve years, and a little longer couldn't have made too much difference; but a twelve-year-old girl was dying, and the situation had been critical. While Jesus was still speaking to the woman, tragic news arrived: Jairus' daughter had died! The messengers saw no need for Jairus to bother Jesus any further. However, Jesus overheard the news and ignored the fact of death. "Ignoring" (v. 36) may also be translated "overhearing." In the context of this verse, both thoughts seem to be true. Jesus was ready to risk his whole reputation by going on with the purpose of healing the girl. Jesus told Jairus to stop being afraid and to keep on believing. Faith was Jesus' prescription for Jairus' worst fear. Faith in Jesus is always the answer to fear.

Jesus allowed only Peter, James, and John to go on with Jairus and him. These disciples were the elect of the elect. When they got to Jairus' home, Jesus heard the loud wailing and saw the hysteria that accompanied the professional mourners who were already announcing the girl's death. These mourners knew death when they saw it, so they laughed Jesus to scorn when he said that the girl was asleep and not dead. Though the girl was dead, Jesus knew that the term did not fit her because she would soon be alive again. The parents were the only real mourners, so Jesus excluded the hired mourners. What a contrast the quiet anticipation must have been as Jesus, his disciples, and the parents went to the girl's body.

The tender words of the Aramaic which Jesus spoke have been preserved for us. Jesus said, "Talitha cumi" (v. 41), telling the little girl to arise. The girl immediately awoke and got up and walked. What had been a house of death came alive with joy and gladness and amazement. Jesus commanded secrecy about the event and told the family to get the girl something to eat. The secrecy was supposedly to keep the crowds from hindering his work. The call for food was a sign that the girl was not only alive but well and hungry.

No Power Over Unbelief (6:1–6)

Jesus and his disciples returned to Nazareth of Galilee. Although Nazareth is not mentioned in these verses, Mark had already referred to Nazareth as the home of Jesus (see 1:9,24). When the sabbath came, Jesus naturally appeared at the synagogue to teach. Despite the criticism Jesus faced there, he did not desert the synagogues (see John 18:20). Jesus taught in the open air and everywhere he went, but it was his custom to be in the synagogue on the sabbath.

The people were amazed at Jesus' wisdom and his mighty works, but their amazement turned into contempt instead of admiration (Mark 6:2–3). They refused to accept him for who he was—namely, the Messiah. They refused to look upon him with faith because he had been one of them: a carpenter, the son of Mary, and the brother to her other children. The people of Nazareth knew Jesus' trade, and they knew his family. Their familiarity with Jesus should have led to admiration; instead, it bred contempt. They would not accept Jesus as fully man and fully God.

Believing people everywhere had marveled at the power of Jesus, but here Jesus marveled at the unbelief of the people (v. 6). Unbelief was a barrier to the exercise of Jesus' power, so Jesus did no powerful work there. The problem was not really Jesus' inability to exercise power and perform miracles in the absence of faith (see 4:35–41). The circumstances made it inappropriate for Jesus to do powerful deeds. The people had been amazed at Jesus' mighty works (6:2); their unspoken doctrine against a common man possibly being the Messiah caused them to stumble in their faith and to be repelled by Jesus. And Jesus would not do a mighty work (6:5) in the absence of faith and in the presence of those who willfully rejected him. While Jesus always answered faith with power, he never forced his power on anyone. So Jesus was able to heal only a few sick people in Nazareth. He has some blessings for us that we will never get unless we trust in him and ask for those blessings in faith.

Verse 4 was probably a current proverb, and the proverb proved true in Jesus' case. Jesus was misunderstood by his own family (until later); he did not receive the honor due him in his own village; and his own country rejected him. As Jesus continued to teach his disciples by word and actions, he left the people who would not receive the good news; and he went to teach in other towns.

Reflection (4:35 to 6:6)

If all the individuals touched by the power of Jesus in these verses of the Bible (4:35 to 6:6) could sing a mighty hymn, their parts would be ready-made: power over nature! power over demons! power over disease! power over death! But the hymn would have to end in a minor key and with a discord: no power over unbelief!

These passages have focused on just about everything that could bring fear to a person. We have seen individuals afraid, unable to control themselves, almost hopeless with disease, and hopeless in death. And we have seen, in contrast and welcome relief to man's anxiety and need, the mighty power of Jesus bring calm, wholeness, and life.

Miracles are still a mystery. No one knows why God doesn't serve up a miracle every time we order one. But perhaps we overlook many of God's miracles, for he is still working his will and responding to people of faith. No one would deny that there are people of faith who die or suffer. But many people do not see God working a miracle through the skilled hands of a surgeon or the mind of a scientist. And, then, God still works in mysterious ways that are beyond our understanding but should not be beyond our belief.

God still has power. What people need is faith, for God has the power to meet every individual's need in the way that God knows is best.

Then Jesus went once more to preach in the villages of Galilee. According to Mark, this was the third time Jesus went on such a preaching mission in Galilee (see 1:14,39).

Commissioned to Serve
6:7–56

After the disciples' calling, they continued to follow Jesus throughout his earthly ministry. However, Mark 6 tells about a time when the disciples went out from Jesus to serve as he had served. When this period of intern apostleship was over, the disciples returned to Jesus because they had much more to learn before Jesus could issue the Great Commission.

Trained for Service (6:7–13)

Jesus had called the disciples to be with him for training and to go out from him for service (see 3:14–15). The order of discipleship has never changed: First, Jesus calls to discipleship; then an individual chooses to become a trained disciple of Jesus; and ultimately that training grows into service for Jesus. Of course, in one sense service begins immediately; but what we are talking about is mature discipleship, which calls for training.

The first commission (v. 7).—The first commission might be termed an in-service-training assignment. The mission came in the middle of the disciples' training period. It was a test mission for Jesus to check on the progress of his disciples, and it was also an opportunity to prepare them for future missions. Jesus had chosen the twelve to multiply his ministry and to continue his work after his death and resurrection.

Jesus divided the twelve into twos and gave them power for the work that lay ahead. The word for *sending* is the verb form for apostle. The sending was a commissioning that authorized the disciples to speak and heal in behalf of Jesus. The disciples were to have the authority of the one who sent them. They were Jesus' ambassadors. Jesus made a practice of sending disciples out in twos and not alone. Jewish custom and Scripture required that there be two witnesses to a truth (see Num. 35:30; Deut. 17:6). Also, going by twos, the disciples could cover more ground than if they went as a company of twelve. One disciple would provide strength for the other, and they would avoid either too much concentration or too much isolation. So the pairs of disciples were to go out with special power over unclean spirits.

Marching orders (vv. 8–11).—A paraphrase may show the simplicity of Jesus' orders to the departing missionaries: "Wear only what you have on, and depend on the hospitality of others." The disciples were commissioned to march with urgency and on faith. They were to travel light like combat soldiers on a short mission. Later, there would be the need to take along provisions for their long mission (see Luke 22:35–36). But even today Christians should not become tied up with worldly concerns that hinder their immediate response to Jesus.

Looking at the orders more closely, we see that a walking stick and sandals were necessary equipment for traveling. But a traveler's bag, food, money, and extra clothes were excess baggage for disciples of faith. Hospitality was a sacred duty in the Middle East, and the disciples were to expect reasonable support in return for their ministry. They were commissioned to give all they had to give and to take whatever hospitality was provided. Their lack of worldly possessions would be in stark contrast to the spiritual riches they had to share with the people who would receive them. The disciples were to accept whatever hospitality was offered to them; they were not to be ungrateful by accepting any offer of better accommodations.

As part of their training, the disciples would learn that not everyone would welcome them and listen to their good news (v. 11). If the disciples and their message were rejected, they were to shake off the dust of their feet. This Jewish custom was a symbolic way of regarding as heathen a people and a place. The act shows that a person did not even have the dust of the road in common with his rejecters. However, shaking off dust was not a curse, but a testimony (or warning) to the inhospitable people (as some commentators and Bible translations point out). Such an action could cause further thought and lead to repentance. And there is a missionary principle here: No one has a right to hear good news a second time until everyone has had a chance to hear it the first time. (See Acts 13:51 for an example.)

Orders followed (vv. 12–13).—The disciples took Jesus' message, not their opinions, to the people. The message was the unchanging message of repentance (see 1:15). When a person repents, he admits his wrong; he changes his mind; and he fits his actions to that change of mind. The disciples also took Jesus' mercy with them. They relieved misery by expelling demons and by healing the sick. Jesus was always concerned about the whole person. Oil was considered a cure-all in those days, and the disciples did what they could in a physical way as well as using the powers that Jesus had given them. Some scholars note that oil was symbolic of the Holy Spirit's presence and suggest that it was used as a sign of divine healing. (See Isa. 1:6 and Jas. 5:14 as references to oil being used in healing.)

Between verses 13 and 30, there is an interlude that gives the effect of time passing while the disciples were gone; and, further, the interlude is used to explain the fate of John the Baptist.

A Commission Fulfilled (6:14–29)

Herod's fears (vv. 14–16).—Jesus' fame spread and multiplied as the six pairs of disciples went about preaching and healing. There were three popular speculations about who Jesus might be: (1) a resurrected John the Baptist, (2) a reappearing Elijah, or (3) a thus-saith-the-Lord prophet (like the prophets of old). What Herod heard about Jesus reminded him of John the Baptist (though John had done no miracle when he was alive—see John 10:41). John had witnessed to Jesus (Mark 1:7–8); and to Herod, Jesus was a resurrected John the Baptist. Herod's guilt-ridden conscience chose this speculation about the person of Jesus. Why?

A flashback (vv. 17–29).—The infamous story of John's death is familiar to almost everyone who knows anything about the Bible, but the underlying cause of John's death needs to come to the surface. John had boldly denounced the adulterous, incestuous marriage between Herodias and Herod Antipas. Herodias was both a sister-in-law and a niece to Herod Antipas. She had been the wife of his brother, Philip. Herod was a king only in the broadest sense of the term. Actually, he was tetrarch of Galilee and Perea, which meant that he ruled one-fourth of the country (compare Mark 6:14 with Matt. 14:1 and Luke 9:7).

John had been commissioned to preach the truth and to call for repentance, so he had repeatedly told Herod that it was not right for him to be living with his brother's wife. The condemnation disturbed Herod, but he would not repent. Herodias literally "had it in" for John (a literal translation of Mark 6:19). John's faith produced fear in Herod, so he would not kill John; but because of Herodias' grudge against John, Herod imprisoned John. Interestingly enough, the faith that overcomes fear for Christians can produce fear in those who resist the Christians.

Herod had a birthday and threw a wild party. Herodias' daughter (said to be Salome) danced what seemingly was a lewd dance that pleased Herod and his important guests. Then Herod promised to give Salome anything up to the half of his kingdom. This was a proverbial statement to express generosity and did not mean that Herod would literally give her half his kingdom. She consulted with her mother and then told Herod she wanted the head of John the Baptist. So on Herod's birthday he had John murdered. John would not desert his divine commission. He lived for truth and died for truth: a mission fulfilled!

The voice of repentance has to be dealt with. People have to respond with repentant lives, or they feel compelled to escape the condemnation—even if they have to silence the voice. Herod had made a rash promise that he kept. It is important to avoid rash promises, but the right moral choice is far more important than losing face.

John was no longer there to teach his disciples or to be followed by them. His disciples buried him. But what John had taught was still alive, and the one he had pointed to would be alive eternally. The fulfillment of John's commission challenges us to invest our lives for the same purpose.

A Missionary Debriefing (6:30–32)

Verse 30 resumes where verse 13 left off. The apostles returned from their mission. At this time the word apostle simply meant one sent on a mission, so the word was roughly equal to our term *missionary*. The disciples had a testimony meeting as they told what they had taught and what they had done. Though we do not know all that the disciples reported, we can sense the enthusiasm that they brought back from their first solo mission.

Because of the disciples' fatigue and because of the heavy two-way traffic of people, Jesus suggested a spiritual retreat. So they set sail for a quiet, restful place across the lake. Jesus was training his disciples to guard against too much constant activity and also against too much withdrawal. There is a time for rest, a time for training, and a time for the battle of service.

Commission and Compassion (6:33–34)

The only rest Jesus and the disciples got, however, was on the boat as it crossed the sea. It was about four miles across the lake (where Jesus and the disciples crossed) and about ten miles around the lake on foot. When Jesus and his disciples got off the boat, they were met by the fleet-footed crowd who had beaten them to their place of retreat. The quest for quietness that would balance the rhythm of life's activity with rest was denied Jesus and his disciples.

Instead of being annoyed, Jesus felt compassion for the people. His compassion for others always had priority over his own personal needs. Jesus had fatigue but not compassion fatigue. Therefore, Jesus began to serve as the shepherd of those people who must have reminded him of shepherdless sheep: They were unable to find their way, unable to find pasture and food, and unable to defend themselves against the dangers which threatened. Jesus gave the disciples a picture of the pastoral role of caring for people. The crowds wanted what Jesus alone could give, and Jesus did not disappoint them.

Concern and Convenience (6:35–44)

Jesus taught the crowds until the afternoon grew late. Then the disciples advised the Master Teacher to send the crowd away so the crowd could buy food for themselves in the village. When people have a need, we tend to express one of two attitudes: (1) Let them take care of themselves, or (2) let's do something about their need. Jesus startled his disciples with the second attitude: "You give them something to eat" (v. 37). The disciples answered, in effect, "We couldn't make enough money in six whole months to feed this crowd one meal" (v. 37). A denarius (or pennyworth) was what a laborer made in a day (see Matt. 20:2). So two hundred denarii worth of bread would cost more than six months' wages.

Jesus was concerned about the people, and the disciples were concerned about convenience. The disciples had obviously forgotten the power that had come with their commission to serve. They also needed to realize that Jesus could use and multiply whatever they had for whatever need existed.

Nevertheless, the disciples agreed to find how much food was available. They found five barley rolls or loaves (see John 6:9) and two fish (perhaps about the size of sardines). Then Jesus, through the disciples, commanded the people to sit down in rectangular companies of hundreds and fifties. Jesus blessed the food, broke it, and gave it to his disciples for distribution. Miraculously, there was enough food for five thousand men (not counting women and children who ate) and twelve baskets left over. What a lesson for the disciples to learn about the power available to them through their commission! And what a lesson for us to become aware that Jesus' power comes with our commission also!

There are those who try to reason away the miracle. This miracle is the only one contained in all four Gospels. The Gospel reporters testified to a creative miracle. As other writers have pointed out, those who argue against miracles do so because they have a doctrine against them; those who testify to miracles do so because they have experienced them. Each person is free to believe what he will. The truth of the matter is that when we give Jesus what little we have, he is always able to make it enough.

An Unlearned Lesson (6:45–52)

Jesus quickly ordered his disciples to sail while he dismissed the crowd. John 6:15 reveals that the people were about to crown Jesus as an earthly king. That would have been a premature and perverted crowning. Surely Jesus didn't want his disciples caught up in such plans because he was training them to tell about a kingdom won by death on the cross and victory over the grave. Jesus refused to be the kind of Messiah the crowd wanted. Then Jesus abruptly withdrew to a hillside to pray about God's will.

Later, while Jesus was looking out across the sea, he saw his disciples rowing but going almost nowhere against the wind. The night was divided into four watches that went from 6:00 P.M. to 6:00 A.M. The fourth watch was between 3:00 A.M. and 6:00 A.M. So about 3:00 A.M. Jesus walked on the water toward the disciples. Some have suggested that Jesus pretended he would pass by the boat to test the faith of the disciples (v. 48). However, "He meant to pass by them" (v. 48) may be translated "He wanted to come alongside them." Both interpretations are possible, but the latter one seems to best fit Jesus' purpose for walking on the water. (It is worth noting that fear and lack of faith go together; see 4:35–41; 5:36; 6:49–50.) Jesus came because of the disciples' need, so it was not his ultimate plan to pass them by.

When the disciples saw Jesus walking on the water, they thought he was a ghost. They were terrified with fear. Jesus identified himself immediately and told his disciples to be courageous and not be afraid. Most translations render verse 50 with "It is I." The literal translation is "I am." That was the name God had used to identify himself to Moses (see Ex. 3:14). The same words appear over and over again in John's Gospel: 4:26; 8:24,28,58; 13:19; 18:5,6,8. But in each of those instances, they are translated, "I am *he*" (the word *he* is supplied). Jesus was trying to help his disciples see that he was the Messiah. As Jesus spoke his soothing words and came to the boat, both the wind and the fear of the disciples were calmed. Whenever Jesus comes, storms have a way of leaving; and whenever faith comes, fear has a way of leaving.

The disciples were dumbfounded. They should have realized that the one who created bread could also walk on water. They had seen the surface facts of the feeding of the five thousand, but they had failed to see that the miracle pointed beyond itself to who Jesus was— the Messiah. They had not been sensitive to the meanings that underlay Jesus' actions. In this way, they were still dull, slow, and immature in their faith; and in this sense, their hearts were hardened (v. 52). Nevertheless, they were more impressed with Jesus than they had ever been before, and they worshiped him as the "Son of God" (see Matt. 14:33).

Part of the training of the twelve was a constant testing and deliverance. They were commissioned, but they still had a lesson to learn. And many modern-day disciples still have a lesson to learn about the miraculous powers of the living Christ.

Selfless Service (6:53–56)

Jesus had directed the disciples to Bethsaida at the northeastern shore of the Sea of Galilee, but the storm interrupted the plans. After the storm, they landed at Gennesaret on the western shore of the

Sea of Galilee. (The Sea of Gennesaret was another name for the Sea of Galilee.) As they drew to the shore and got out, the crowds immediately recognized Jesus.

People knew their needs, and they recognized that Jesus would heal those who were determined to grasp the opportunity of his presence. The healing sounded like earlier instances in his ministry. The lame were carried on pallets, and others struggled to touch the fringe of Jesus' garments. A trusting touch was enough; many were healed (contrast this picture with Mark 6:5). People always wanted what Jesus had to give, but what a joy it would have been to him if people had come with what they had to give. But Jesus' tireless, selfless service was a lesson for the student-disciples to learn and follow.

Another way of stating the heart of Mark 6 is this: The work of Jesus has to be carried on in the world by commissioned followers, and training is necessary for effective performance of this work. In the deep part of our souls, all of us need to ask God what he wants us to do with our lives. Then we need to be willing to train for the mission.

Religion That Is Real
7:1–23

The open and honest ministry of Jesus illuminated truth. It also acted as an all-revealing light that exposed the Pharisees and the farce that many of them had made of religion. Jesus made plain the characteristics of both real and unreal religion. He did this by pointing out the errors of his critics and by putting in proper perspective God's intentions and man-made traditions.

Man-made Religion (7:1–8)

The Pharisees and scribes hovered over Jesus and his disciples like vultures, waiting for a chance to make their cowardly attack. Some of the disciples opened the door to conflict when they ate without ceremonially washing their hands. This act meant that the disciples had eaten with impure hands, according to the tradition of the elders.

Verses 3–4 serve as a parenthetical footnote for the Gentile (non-Jewish) readers of Mark's Gospel to explain the reason for conflict. The religious leaders promptly condemned the disciples. Now the people of those days didn't know anything about germs; their concern was not for hygiene but for religion. Had the disciples really done anything that was wrong?

"The tradition of the elders" (v. 3) tried to spell out in meticulous detail the written law of God. From the time of Moses on, esteemed ancestors had multiplied the interpretations of certain ceremonial laws (see Lev. 11–15; 22:6; Num. 19). This practice had especially developed since the fourth and fifth century B.C. Whenever the Scriptures were silent or unspecific on some question, these elders laid down a ruling, which in time was considered equal in rank with God's Word. (In this context, *elder* does not seem to refer to age but to those who interpreted the law.) The Pharisees and scribes eventually began to determine proper religion primarily by the tradition of the elders. The result approached a man-made religion that worshiped tradition instead of worshiping God. Strange as it may seem, some people still rely on historical positions when these traditional views may be distortions of God's Word.

Pharisees meant separated ones. In the beginning, Pharisees had tried to separate themselves from anything unholy or polluted so that they would be fit to serve God. So the original motive was good. And in fairness to the religious leaders and their criticism, the serious Bible student should study the ceremonial law and some of the reasons for its existence. The Israelites were set aside to be God's chosen people. Anything that would hinder that calling was forbidden because it would make them spiritually unclean. So, instead of thinking in terms of dirt and germs, we should contrast *clean* and *holy* with *unclean* and *unholy* (see Lev. 10:10).

In their efforts to be separate, religious leaders had failed to understand that duty to God and duty to man go together in real religion. They had also failed to understand that the condition of a person's heart toward God and man is the basis for God to judge a person as being holy. No amount of separation from the unholy can make us holy. No outer separation can rid the inner pollution of resentment, bitterness, jealousy, grudges, pride, and other sins of attitude. Outward behavior can be a symptom of a person's spiritual condition, but the condition of the heart is the crucial element in being clean and holy.

This background and these truths are helpful in understanding Mark 7:1–8.

Because of the tradition of the elders, a strict Jew observed ritual handwashing before each meal. And upon return from the supposedly Gentile-contaminated marketplace, a strict Jew would wash his whole body. Real religion was buried beneath such minute rules of tradition. And that kind of rule was applied to Jesus' disciples when they ate with unwashed hands.

When the religious leaders confronted Jesus with the charge of broken tradition on the part of some of his disciples, Jesus responded with the charge that the Pharisees and scribes were hypocrites who substituted man-made religion for God-given commandments. In quoting from Isaiah 29:13, Jesus revealed that the Pharisees' and scribes' religion was just a play, a put-on, make-believe religion. Whatever their original motives had been—knowingly or unknowingly— the Pharisees and scribes had moved away from genuine religion. They talked a good case of religion, but they did not live one. Their lives proved that the outside can look perfect while the inside is rotten. Perhaps all of us are guilty of hypocrisy at different times and in different ways. This truth stands: Religious observances are to be expressions of real religion and not awkward interludes in lives that practice sin.

Jesus came as God's gift of grace to make mankind clean and holy. The ceremonial law of the Old Testament was to be fulfilled in Jesus. And the man-made laws that did not carry out God's intention should never have been in the first place. No, the disciples were not wrong.

Religious Travesty (7:9–13)

By citing a specific example, Jesus continued his attack against man-made rules that contradicted the command of God. Exodus 20:12 and 21:17 clearly showed that a person was responsible for his parents (see also Mark 7:10). Yet, the religious lawyers had invented a mythical loophole for commandment-evasion. According to the Pharisees and scribes, children could free themselves from parental responsibility by declaring whatever they had to help their parents with as *Corban*. *Corban* was a Hebrew word that was used in the last centuries B.C. and the first century A.D. in a dedication formula. The word was used in the Old Testament to indicate a gift to God. During Jesus' earthly ministry, *Corban* was used by the Pharisees and scribes and their followers to indicate the setting aside of something as a gift to God or as a Temple gift.

Scholars are uncertain about all that was involved in saying *Corban*. However, in this context, they agree on the heart of the matter. Those who uttered *Corban* were telling their parents that any support they had counted on was withdrawn because the support was vowed as a gift to God. God comes before parents. But somehow the children would still have use of the money. Perhaps the gift involved a will or trust. Either way, the practice was tradition, not God's law.

According to Jesus, the ruling of the religious leaders seemingly would be that the oath of the gift could not be undone no matter what happened to the parents. So the main point is clear: Even if the money was set aside for religious use only (as the Jewish word *Corban* supposedly indicated), such a vow would mock true religion and would deny the Fifth Commandment (Ex. 20:12) that indicated God's will about parents.

Legalistically, the vow would carry out the letter of the law stated in Numbers 30:1–2, but it would at the same time put a man-made vow over a God-given law. The lawyers and their traditions had missed the spirit of the law and had perverted what God intended in the law (see Deut. 5:16; Lev. 20:9).

They had talked about "the tradition of the elders" (Mark 7:5); Jesus responded by referring to "the precepts of men" (v. 7), "the tradition of men" (v. 8), "your tradition" (v. 9), and "your tradition" (v. 13). The light of judgment upon those who had distorted God's law must have gotten higher and more glaring with each statement that pointed to Jesus' listeners.

Jesus took the example of *Corban* as just one of many examples he could have used. And religion like that—religion that lets man put tradition before God's commandments—cannot be real religion.

In his *Dogmatics* (2/2, p. 647), Karl Barth has expressed well the relationship that should exist between tradition and Scripture: "The Church is most faithful to its tradition, and realizes its unity with the Church of every age, when, linked but not tied by its past, it to-day searches the Scriptures and orientates its life by them as though this had to happen to-day for the first time." Tradition must stand the test of being submitted to the Scriptures!

Religious Reality (7:14–23)

The Pharisees and scribes had charged that Jesus' disciples had done wrong by eating with ceremonially unclean hands (v. 5). Jesus had answered the religious leaders by condemning their hypocrisy. Now he turned from the Pharisees to teach the crowd about real religion and the reason his disciples were not wrong.

Jesus told the people that real religion shows up in what a person thinks and does, not in what he eats and touches. He was saying that persons may be spiritually impure but not things. That fact shattered the Jewish ceremonial system and even left Jesus' own disciples puzzled (v. 17). Jesus simply explained that the digestive system takes care of all food (vv. 18–19), and the heart gives birth to evil ideas and actions. In other words, what defiles a person is a foul imagination and evil attitudes; and these inner wrongs express themselves in evil actions that Jesus listed as examples.

The truth is that God knows and judges a person by his heart (1 Sam. 16:7; Luke 16:15), not by his diet. In reality, the only cure for sin's real source, therefore, is to purify the heart. And that purification takes place only when a person turns his heart and his life over to God. Man doesn't need a better heart; he needs a new heart (see 1 Sam. 10:9 as an example of a new heart that indicates God's gift of a new attitude).

These verses are not a license to take into the body anything that might harm it. Jesus was simply pointing out that personal defilement is spiritual, not mechanical and legalistic. The act of defilement is the outcome of a defiled heart.

Faith That Brings a Response
7:24 to 8:26

Jesus went from the cold criticism of unbelieving religious leaders to the warm faith of those who needed him. The journey is interesting because of the mixture of attitudes toward Jesus and the responses each attitude brought.

A Unique Faith (7:24–30)

For all practical purposes, Jesus' Galilean ministry was over, and he went to the region of Tyre and Sidon. This withdrawal began an extensive circular journey that was the longest recorded trip Jesus made. (See a map to get the picture.) Jesus quietly entered a house because he wanted and needed privacy and rest. But people in the region of Tyre and Sidon already knew about Jesus' power to heal (see 3:8), and it was futile for him to try to hide. A Greek-speaking Syrophoenician woman had such a great need that she invaded Jesus' privacy. Her daughter was possessed by an unclean spirit or demon. In this case the Bible doesn't tell what the symptoms of disorder were. But we can imagine that they were something like those described in Mark 9:14–29. Whatever the symptoms were, they had caused the mother deep anguish; and she believed that Jesus could heal the daughter.

Jesus did not refuse to heal the daughter, but he tested the woman's faith by telling her that it was not right to feed the puppies before feeding the children. Most commentators understand *dogs* to refer to Gentiles and *children* to refer to Israelites (also see Matt. 15:24). It is true that Jewish people often referred to Gentiles as dogs (see Isa. 56:10–11). The term was a symbol of dishonor and contempt then even as it is today. The woman didn't say, "What do you mean?" And she may not have understood Jesus to be speaking about Jews and non-Jews. Perhaps she just took Jesus' words literally. Anyone who has little children knows that there will be food on the floor at mealtime; and if the children have puppies, they will be eating the crumbs that fall on the floor.

The test Jesus put to the woman may have been softened by Jesus' tone of voice, kindness in his eyes, and his term "puppies" (in the original language). Regardless of how stern the test was, the mother's faith persisted in recognizing Jesus as Lord and in pointing out the custom of dogs eating what the children dropped. The humble woman did not bristle, but she said, in effect, "Just give my daughter a crumb of your healing power." Jesus immediately pronounced the daughter healed because of the woman's expression of faith. In faith the woman responded to Jesus' command; she went home and found her daughter healed. This miracle was a rare instance of Jesus healing someone at a distance.

What made the woman's faith unique was that she would not take no for an answer. Her religion was real. From her example, we learn these truths: Faith that brings a response recognizes Jesus as Lord; the heart's motive is right; the person is willing to risk humiliation out of unselfish concern; and the faith will persist until there is an answer.

Faithful Friends (7:31–37)

Jesus traveled from the region of Tyre to the Sea of Galilee, and the route he chose raises curiosity and causes speculation. He went north to Sidon and back down through the Decapolis to the Sea of Galilee. Mark stated the trip in a sentence, but it undoubtedly took Jesus several weeks. Commentators suppose that Jesus took the wandering trip to stay away from Herod for the time being and to continue to teach his disciples.

The people in the ten Greek cities known as the Decapolis were largely Gentiles, but there were also Jews in those cities; so we are not completely sure about the makeup of the people who came to meet Jesus. Whoever the people were, some of them were friends of a man who was deaf and had a speech impediment. They wanted Jesus to lay his hands on the man—for blessing or healing or both.

Jesus took the man aside and privately pantomimed with divine sign language the healing that would take place. Since the man could not hear, he would not hear the command of healing. Although we do not read that the man had faith, he and his friends came with a faith that did not need to be recorded. Their presence spoke for them. After Jesus had touched the man's ears and placed the saliva on his tongue, he was ready to pray. The Jews and Greeks felt that spittle had curative powers, so these actions of Jesus may have reinforced the man's faith. Then Jesus looked to heaven, sighed, and spoke the Aramaic or Hebrew word *Ephphatha*, which meant, "Be opened!" Instantly, the man could hear and speak clearly.

For anyone versed in the Old Testament, the miracle would have been a reminder of Isaiah 35:4–6, which gave a preview of the Messiah's healing actions. Jesus, the Messiah, had graciously removed the physical barriers to communication. If the healed man was a Gentile, Jesus' actions showed that nationality was never a barrier to his concern. In fact, some scholars believe that this was Jesus' way of showing that there were no unclean people, just as there was no unclean food (in a ceremonial sense).

Jesus asked the crowd not to tell anyone what had happened (v. 36; see also 1:44; 5:18–20). They did just the opposite of what Jesus asked. Jesus expressed his messiahship in his own way and in terms that were best for the people. If he were constantly crowded by people who treated him only as a miracle worker, he would be hindered in his preaching and in his training of the disciples.

Verse 37 has been described as a Gentile hallelujah. The words of amazement and praise echo the words of Genesis 1:31. Jesus responded to faith by healing in a way that made people much more nearly what they were created to be.

Faith at Work (8:1–10)

The next scene pictured four thousand people in the desert with nothing to eat. They had been with Jesus for three days, and they had run out of provisions. The time must have been one of intensive teaching. This time Jesus called the need for food to the attention of his disciples. To the disciples, lack of food for four thousand people in a desert place was a calamity. But to the compassionate Jesus, the need of people was always a challenge to be met. And just as Jesus had fed the five thousand (6:30–44), he also fed the four thousand. The circumstances were similar, but the numbers were different. Some people wonder whether there was just one miracle of feeding the multitudes, but Mark 8:19–20 clearly speaks against such a viewpoint. And the details offer a good bit of difference.

In this incident, there were four thousand people, seven loaves and a few fish, and seven baskets left over. The baskets left over were large enough to hold a man in (v. 8), while in the earlier feeding the baskets were small (6:43). The first feeding was presumably to the Jews, and the second feeding was primarily to Gentiles; but in both cases, Jesus saw the need of human beings, and he had a compassion that actively cared for their need. In both instances, Jesus took small resources and did great things with them; and both times he expected the disciples to serve the multitudes. By example, Jesus showed that faith is never more real than when it is at work helping people in need.

After Jesus dismissed the crowd, he went from the Decapolis area to Dalmanutha. It is now difficult to identify Dalmanutha. The best guess we have is to identify it with Magdala, but it will take more research than we now have to prove this identification. The location was probably on the western shore of Galilee.

A Faithless Request (8:11–13)

Some Pharisees challenged Jesus to give them a sign. They tempted Jesus to prove his messiahship or source of authority through some visible proof. In essence, they were saying, "We will accept your authority as being from God if you will prove it our way." Earlier he had performed a miracle before the religious rulers (3:22–30), but they had attributed the miracle to the devil. The Pharisees were not looking for a display of power as much as they were looking for some evidence that would prove the source of power. Jesus came to call people to faith, but the faithless Pharisees insisted on a special sign (see Deut. 18:18–22 for background). Their motive was not a desire to believe in Jesus but a desire to discredit him (Mark 8:11).

With deep despair Jesus absolutely refused to give the kind of sign the Pharisees wanted. His life and ministry were enough for those who really wanted to believe. The only sign he would give would be the sign of Jonah (see Matt. 12:39–42; 16:4; Luke 11:29–30). Jesus' death, burial, and resurrection would be the ultimate sign to verify that Jesus was the Messiah. In the meantime, those spiritually blinded Pharisees lacked real religion's essential ingredient of faith (see 1 Cor. 1:22–23). When the motive is wrong and faith is absent, demands do not bring a response.

Experience: a Basis for Faith (8:14–21)

Shortly after the Pharisees had asked Jesus for a sign, Jesus told his disciples to guard against the leaven of the Pharisees and the leaven of Herod (v. 15). Leaven was yeast, and it symbolized moral influence whether good or bad. However, more often than not, it stood for bad (see Matt. 16:6; Luke 12:1); and it stood for evil in verse 15. A seemingly insignificant amount of yeast could spread through a much larger amount of dough. Fresh from the encounter with the Pharisees, Jesus seemed to be telling his disciples not to let the evil thinking of the Pharisees and Herod (or the Herodians) contaminate their own faith. In Mark 3:6 the Pharisees and Herodians had plotted together to destroy Jesus, so some interpreters think the reference to Herod really was a reference to the Herodians. On the other hand, both the Pharisees and Herod had wanted Jesus to produce a sign (Mark 8:11; Luke 23:8). Jesus did help people in need, but he was calling them to faith apart from signs like those the Pharisees and Herod wanted.

Jesus and his disciples had left the encounter with the Pharisees abruptly (Mark 8:13), and the disciples had forgotten to get a supply of bread. When Jesus mentioned leaven, the disciples took Jesus' symbolic language literally and became preoccupied with food. They said they had no bread (v. 16), but they did have one loaf of bread (v. 14). Amazed, Jesus chided his disciples for their lack of understanding and for their unnecessary concern about food. They had failed to understand what it meant to have the presence of Jesus with them. Jesus surely had not chosen his disciples because they were quick learners (see Mark 4:13,40; 6:52; 7:18; 8:17–18). They were insensitive to the fact that Jesus had proved he was sufficient for every emergency. But sometimes slow learners learn well; and when they learn, they become faithful people who live their convictions. That kind of understanding was near for the disciples.

Jesus had provided for his disciples' need in the past (vv. 19–20), and was that not a guarantee that Jesus would provide for the future? Jesus had intended to instruct his disciples in faithfulness that did not depend on earthly power or visible signs like those the Pharisees and Herod wanted. But because of the disciples' misunderstanding, an underlying lesson came out: Past experiences with Jesus should increase spiritual understanding and faith in the present and in the future. Christians are expected to grow in their religious faith.

A Response to Faith (8:22–26)

After so many examples of spiritual blindness, Jesus healed a man who was physically blind. Some people of faith brought the blind man to Jesus for his touch that would heal.

Jesus led the man away from the crowds and out of the village of Bethsaida. The blind man's willingness to let Jesus lead him called for steps of faith on the part of the blind man. Then Jesus took saliva and put it on the man's eyes; and like a physician, Jesus said, "Do you see anything?" (v. 23). The healing was only partial. The man reported seeing something like all of us very nearsighted people have experienced when we try to see without our glasses. He looked beyond

Jesus and saw men that appeared to be walking trees (v. 24). Jesus gave the man's eyes a second touch that cured even the nearsightedness or fuzziness; the man could then see clearly at a distance.

This incident was much like the healing of the man with the speech impediment (7:31–37). This miracle was done in private and spittle was used, but it was unique in that the healing came gradually in two stages instead of coming instantly. Jesus told the man to go home without even entering the village. The reason for this instruction may have been for secrecy (see v. 26, KJV), or it may not have been (v. 26, RSV). No one knows for sure.

Jesus can enable the spiritually blind to see. As a matter of fact, all of life is a gradual miracle for the ones who have real faith and real religion; for God unfolds his truths to us and helps us to have a vibrant and meaningful faith that brings response.

Religion that is real and faith that brings response are shown by having a proper relationship with God; they are further expressed by righteousness that stems from a pure heart and unselfish concern that cares for the needs of others. Jesus' life is the model and essence of one whose religion is genuine and whose faith is powerful. No matter how others may think and live, we are responsible for having the mind of Christ and living the life he lived in our attitudes and actions.

Messiahship and Discipleship
8:27 to 9:50

Mark 8:27 divides the entire book of Mark. Up to this point in the book, the emphasis has been upon Jesus' ministry. From Mark 8:27 onward, the note of Jesus' suffering meets us at every turn. Mark devoted the last half of his book to Jesus' teachings, his approach to the cross, his actual suffering and death, and the resurrection.

Jesus' training of the twelve was not over by any means. But the time had come to test their understanding and to help them get a fuller picture of messiahship and discipleship.

Understanding Tested (8:27–30)

From Bethsaida Jesus and his disciples went north about twenty-five miles to the villages around Caesarea Philippi. The city itself was named after Caesar, and it was an area where Caesar was looked upon as lord. Between Bethsaida and Caesarea Philippi, Jesus asked the crucial question that would test all of his teaching and all of the disciples' learning: *Who am I?* Jesus asked this question in two different ways, and even the questioning was a way of further teaching.

Jesus began the questioning about his identity by asking the disciples who other men said he was. Various disciples answered: John the Baptist, Elijah, or one of the other prophets (Matthew added Jeremiah; see Matt. 16:14). These answers were mentioned earlier in Mark 6:14–29. Most people seemed to believe Jesus was a prophet returned from the dead. But which prophet? All of the speculations about his being a prophet fell short of the truth, for Jesus was much more than a prophet. And the people did not even guess that Jesus could be greater than a prophet. He was the one for whom the prophets had prepared the way by divine commission.

Jesus continued the questioning about his identity. As tension mounted, Jesus asked in so many words, "I know who other men say I am, but now I want to know who *you* believe I am. Who am I?" Like a rifle shot Peter gave the one right answer (and the answer that must have been in the hearts of the other disciples): "You are the Christ." *Christ* was Greek and *Messiah* was Hebrew for the Anointed One. For a Jew to accept Jesus as the Messiah meant accepting him as Lord of lords, King of kings, Prophet of prophets, and Priest of priests—as the Son of God, the long-awaited Deliverer. Peter made the great confession that every Jew had wanted to be able to make: that the Messiah had come!

Jesus did not say yes or no about the great disclosure, but his words showed that he did own up to the messiahship. Jesus did this by blessing Peter for his answer and by saying that the revelation had come from the Father above (see Matt. 16:17–19). If Peter was the primary source of Mark's information, it is worth noting that Peter did not include his blessing here. Either way, the information is missing from Mark.

Messiah was a title and not a name. Although Mark had stated that Jesus was the Messiah in Mark 1:1, the certainty of Jesus' messiahship had not been stated to the disciples before. Religious leaders had attributed Jesus' power to the realm of the demonic. The demons had recognized Jesus as the Messiah, but he had hushed their lips. Undoubtedly, the disciples had suspected his messiahship, reached certain levels of belief, and had perhaps alternated between belief and doubt. As recently as Mark 8:21 Jesus had asked, "Do you not yet understand?" That question demanded an answer, and Peter gave the answer magnificently in Mark 8:29. The answer was the turning point in Mark's unfolding drama of Jesus' messiahship.

Once again Jesus commanded silence about this matter. He still needed to teach his disciples the meaning of messiahship and discipleship. While Peter had gotten the title of Jesus right, his understanding—and that of the other disciples—was incomplete. The Jews were looking for a superman-type of Messiah. And Jesus had to teach his disciples God's will for the Messiah, which was a will that did not match man's understanding of what the Messiah had to do to save man. So because the right time had not come and because Jesus needed to fill his disciples with the full meaning of messiahship, he commanded their silence.

Marks of Messiahship (8:31–33)

Jesus had lived his messiahship before the disciples, and they had been sensitive enough to discover the early signs of it. But gladness turned to sadness when Jesus began to reveal more fully what it meant to be Messiah. It was good for Jesus' disciples to know him as the Messiah, but it was equally important for them to know the title's meaning as Jesus knew it.

In reeducating the disciples about the meaning of discipleship, Jesus referred to himself as "the Son of man" who must suffer, be rejected, die, and rise again. The *must* of verse 31 was God's plan, not a concession to man. From beginning to end Jesus was conscious of a divine plan, and out of divine necessity Jesus would voluntarily obey that plan. This prophecy of Jesus' *suffering* death and resurrection was the first of three times that Jesus would plainly state the prophecy in this way in Mark (8:31; 9:31; 10:33–34). Other references that were veiled or stated differently appear in 2:20; 3:6; 9:9; and 14:28. (Also, see Hos. 6:1–2; Isa. 53; Matt. 16:4; Mark 8:12.)

Because the Jewish people had already decided what the coming

Messiah must be like and what he must do, there was no room in their thinking for a Suffering Servant Messiah. The Jewish idea of how the Messiah would establish his kingdom included military violence that would be destructive and a nationalistic spirit that would be vengeful (compare 2 Sam. 7:14–16 and Jer. 23:5–6 with Isa. 53:3–5).

Even Peter, who had named Jesus as the Messiah, could not accept suffering, rejection, and death as marks of messiahship. Peter seemingly did not hear Jesus' promise of resurrection. So Peter took Jesus to task for such a prediction. The temptation Peter presented to Jesus was messiahship some way other than God's way on the cross. It was the same temptation Satan had used against Jesus in the wilderness (see Matt. 4:1–11; Luke 4:1–13). Consequently, Jesus said, "Get out of my way, Satan! for this view of yours is not from God but from men" (Mark 8:33, Williams). Peter had made the great confession with wisdom from God, but with the weakness of man he would not accept the marks of Messiah as Jesus explained them. (If Peter was Mark's source for this information, notice that while Peter withheld the commendation he got from Jesus, he did not withhold the rebuke he got.)

For Jesus the cost of redemption included not only the constant head-on collision with temptation but also the rebuke of his own disciples. Satan tried to use those closest to Jesus to turn Jesus from the will of God. Being the Messiah cost Jesus everything. But Jesus never failed to live out his total commitment to the will of his Father. Jesus would come to his glory by way of the cross. That fact dominates the rest of the book of Mark; and it immediately speaks to the cost of discipleship.

The Cost of Discipleship (8:34 to 9:1)

After telling what price he would pay for man's redemption, Jesus revealed what it would cost a person who really *wanted* to follow him as the Christ. Verse 34 sets forth three conditions of discipleship: (1) A person must deny himself once and for all. Self-denial does not mean just giving up things; it means giving up self. The purpose for saying no to self is to be able to say yes to God whenever there is a choice involving God's will and some other way. (2) A disciple must take up his cross daily (see Luke 9:23). People carrying crosses in those days were going to their execution; so Jesus' statement meant his disciples had to be willing to forfeit their lives and to be counted as criminals. They had to be willing to live for Jesus, enduring perhaps even the kind of suffering that occurs on a cross. This was Jesus' first mention of the cross, but surely he knew what the cross would mean for him and for his disciples. (3) A disciple has to give continual loyalty to Jesus. These are the conditions of discipleship (or of becoming a Christian and living the Christian life).

Mark's early readers were enduring persecution, and the words of Jesus must have been an encouraging challenge to continue the Christian life in the face of death. Some of them would have the chance of preserving physical life by denying that Jesus was their Lord and by claiming Caesar as their lord. But Jesus had called his disciples to look at the physical and temporary in light of the spiritual and eternal. Jesus talked about profit, loss, gain, saving, forfeiting, and giving in exchange. In modern terminology, we would say that Jesus asked us to count up all the costs of discipleship and then look at the bottom line of return.

Though Jesus' way was the hard choice, it was and is the way to make life great now and forevermore. Such good news is no reason for shame (compare Mark 8:38 with Rom. 1:14-17). What a person does in response to Jesus makes an everlasting difference. The consequences will be disastrous for those who are ashamed of Jesus, unfaithful to him (adulterous), and sinful in their way of life (v. 38). The truth is that a person cannot live for Christ and lose, and he cannot live for self and win. Jesus made it plain that a person has to choose as his supreme value either living for self or living for Christ.

Most scholars think that "the kingdom of God come with power" (9:1) referred to one or more of the following: (1) the transfiguration, (2) the resurrection of Jesus, (3) the gift of the Spirit at Pentecost, and (4) the expansion of the early church. (See Matt. 16:27-28 and Rom. 1:4 for related texts.)

Though there are many suggested interpretations to Mark 9:1, the question about which interpretation is right is still open. And, of course, the full force of the kingdom's power will be at Christ's second coming.

A Glimpse of Glory (9:2-8)

Jesus had promised his disciples he would return in glory after his death; but Peter, James, and John got a preview of that glory in the transfiguration experience. When Jesus was transformed, the disciples literally saw him in a new light of heavenly glory. Then Elijah and Moses reappeared just as mysteriously as they had left the earthly scene. Why those two? Perhaps it was because Moses commonly represented the Law, and Elijah stood for the Prophets. Into that spiritual summit conference came the voice of God to claim Jesus as Son and to approve his ministry (see 1:9–11).

For Jesus, the experience was further preparation for the cross (Luke 9:31) and reassurance of his divine sonship. For Peter, James, and John, the transfiguration was a time of spiritual insight: They fellowshipped with the saints; they saw Jesus in his glory; and they heard God's voice confirm Jesus as the Messiah. Surely this memorable experience strengthened the disciples for what lay ahead of them.

The mountain of transfiguration is not identified, but it could have been Mount Hermon. Although Luke 9:32 tells of the disciples having been asleep and Matthew 17:9 speaks of a vision, the experience was real and the disciples were wide awake when they saw Jesus in his glory. They saw Jesus in a shining brilliance. His clothes were whiter than any fuller could make them. A fuller was one who cleaned and prepared wool.

With Elijah there and Moses, too, Peter must have thought the kingdom had come in its completeness. Whatever he thought, he wanted to build three booths or shelters. But a cloud enclosed Jesus, Elijah, and Moses. And God's voice reaffirmed that Jesus was his divine Son and told the disciples to listen to him. Jesus had said for those with ears to hear (4:9,23; 8:18); now God reinforced that command.

Every Christian has the promise of a future transfiguration. Interestingly enough, the Greek word for *transfigured* (used in v. 2) is applied in Romans 12:1–2 and 2 Corinthians 3:18 to obedient Christians who let God transform their lives.

Redemption's Plan (9:9–13)

The divine plan of redemption once more called for silence about the events surrounding Jesus' messiahship. The planned time for Jesus' disciples to tell all was after Jesus' resurrection. But the doctrine of the resurrection and where Elijah fit in puzzled the disciples who had just seen Moses and Elijah.

With the fresh image of Elijah in their minds, the disciples wanted Jesus to explain the scribes' teaching about the return of Elijah before the coming of the Messiah. Jesus agreed with the scribes' teaching (see Mal. 4:5–6), and he revealed that John the Baptist was Elijah—symbolically speaking (see Matt. 17:11–13). John had fulfilled the role of Elijah in a sense because he had turned people back to God in repentance and forgiveness. John had suffered, and so would Jesus. There would be humiliation before glory.

Faith's Quality (9:14–29)

Once more Jesus descended to the surroundings of frail mankind. The scene was disheartening: powerless disciples, arguing scribes, and a brokenhearted father with an epileptic son. The boy reportedly had an evil spirit, and the symptoms came out in the form of epilepsy. That was the scene when Jesus came down from the glory of the transfiguration. The details of this event contrast messiahship and discipleship.

When Jesus, Peter, James, and John came down to join the other disciples, they were met by the disciples, scribes, and a crowd that seemingly sensed that Jesus would settle an argument. Jesus' question in verse 16 could have been directed to the disciples, the scribes, or the crowd as a whole. Jesus wanted to know what the debate was about. Before a disciple or a scribe could answer the question, a troubled father said, in effect: "I'm responsible. I brought my son to you for healing. You were gone, so I appealed to your disciples who were supposed to have your authority to cast out demons and heal. But they were powerless. That's when the argument began." The argument may have been about how to cast out demons or who had the authority to cast out demons.

The disciples' failure was striking in view of the authority Jesus had given them earlier (see 6:7,13). While Jesus had been gone, the disciples were unable to heal, and they probably were unable to hold their own in a debate with the scribes; so the situation was embarrassing for them. No wonder Jesus was dismayed with the lack of faith of the disciples matched by the unbelief of the crowd. Jesus then ordered the boy to be brought to him (v. 19).

The picture of the demon-possessed boy and his father was pathetic. From childhood the boy had these symptoms: unable to speak and hear (vv. 17–26), convulsed to the ground, foaming at the mouth, grinding his teeth, and rigid or exhausted. Whenever the seizures would come, the boy's life was endangered by the demon's plan of plunging the boy into fire or water. (The image of God was distorted in this person, and Satan would have liked to destroy it altogether.)

For years the boy had required twenty-four-hour watchcare. No wonder the father said, "But if you can do anything, have pity on *us* and help *us*" (v. 22; writer's italics). The implication was, "Your disciples are powerless; but if you have any power, help us!" Jesus immediately set the record straight: His power was not in question; man's lack of faith was the problem (v. 23). The man had had some faith, or he would not have brought his boy to Jesus. But when Jesus pointed to faith as the missing quality, the father didn't argue. He prayed, "I believe; help my unbelief!" (v. 24). Jesus healed the boy once and for all and showed that salvation is for all of life as well as for death. The boy lay as peacefully after the convulsive spirit left him as if he were dead; but Jesus lifted him to life—almost as a preview of final death and resurrection.

Privately, the disciples wanted to know why they hadn't been able to cast out the demon. Though Jesus had grown weary of their lack of faith (v. 19; see also 4:40; 6:50,52; 8:17–21), they were still learners; and he was still their Master Teacher. Jesus explained that this kind of demon could be driven out only by prayers of faith (vv. 19,29). The best Greek manuscripts do not include fasting as a requirement for casting out demons. Jesus did not have to fast to cast out the demon, and he had exempted the disciples from any need to fast while he was with them (see 2:18–22).

The incident proved that only lack of faith and lack of prayer hinder man's full deliverance. When faith is not what it should be, we need to pray for a better quality of faith. Further, a person with real faith will not set a limit on God's power that is available in Jesus.

A Prophetic Promise (9:30–32)

Jesus led his disciples through Galilee, and he wanted to be alone with them because he needed to teach them about his messiahship. In a second major prophecy Jesus tried to impress upon all of his disciples the price and the promise of redemption. In the plan of God and in the obedient decision of Jesus, it was already decided that Jesus would be handed over to men who would kill him. Jesus was teaching his disciples that their fellowship would not end with his death; he would rise after three days to be followed forevermore. Still, the disciples could not grasp Jesus' kind of kingship and his certainty of resurrection. "Son of man" could be used as a synonym for *I,* so that term was not the problem. The disciples didn't understand, and—like so many pupils—they were afraid to ask what they didn't understand. Perhaps they were afraid to find out more than they understood.

Misplaced Commitment (9:33–37)

On the way to Capernaum the disciples had followed Jesus, but they had discussed or argued about commitment to self. Though he knew, Jesus asked what the disciples had been discussing. Their silence was noisy with embarrassment. But Jesus had asked his question to teach them about greatness, so no answer was really necessary on their part. Jesus gathered the disciples around him and sat to teach.

The disciples had argued about who was the greatest. Or in modern terms, they argued about who was No. 1. They had confused greatness with grandness, and they were still committed to selfish goals. Jesus explained that if they wanted to be first and great they had to be last and least. Verse 35 was another way of saying what Jesus had taught in Mark 8:34 about denying self. The disciples were to find that service was the way to greatness.

Jesus hugged a child to him and showed his disciples that being lovable was more important than being great. At the same time, it is a great thing to be humble and without pretense as a child. A second lesson from this acted-out parable was the greatness involved in welcoming children. Adults often try to impress other adults while ignoring children. Jesus' example about greatness should be an encouraging word to those who receive and teach little children about God and his truths. Selfless commitment to others leads to a magnificent commitment to Jesus as we serve in his name. Jesus is to be the object of our commitment, and we are to follow his example in serving others (see Matt. 18:2–5).

Motive—Not Method (9:38–41)

John and the other disciples did not want anyone to use Jesus' name authoritatively to cast out demons unless he joined Jesus' company. In so many words, Jesus told the disciples to test a person's commitment by his motive, not by his method. When a person's methods do not conform to tradition, Jesus would tell us to exercise tolerance. The disciples had not been able to cast out a demon in Mark 9:14–18. Could their concern have been partly an expression of jealousy?

Jesus pointed out that the person who heals in Jesus' name is not against Jesus. The disciples needed to move beyond their narrow viewpoint in understanding. Jesus indicated that any service which helps his cause will bring a blessing in return. If a person casts out a demon in Jesus' name or merely gives a cup of cold water to those who bear the name of Christ, that person shares in the mission of Jesus.

Total Commitment (9:42–50)

Jesus sternly warned his disciples that it would be a tragedy for anyone to trip up any of his children who tried to follow him. Causing others to stumble into sin is a serious offense. Those who teach and influence others have special reason to consider verse 42.

However, sin is a personal choice. Jesus seemed to demand self-mutilation as a cure for sin. That was his way of symbolically calling for self-conquest and total commitment. The truth is this: No matter how radical the act has to be, we must get rid of sin. The alternative to such commitment is condemnation for sin. We might better understand the teaching if we compared it to the decision of a surgeon to remove whatever part of the body threatens the life of the rest of the body for any reason. The cost of discipleship is great, but discipleship is worth the cost. (The RSV omits verses 44 and 46 as do the most ancient manuscripts; but those verses are identical with verse 48, which depicts the awfulness of hell.)

The three salt sayings suggest that Christians are to have purity, zeal, and fellowship (vv. 49–50). Old Testament sacrifices were to be offered with salt (Lev. 2:13; Ezek. 43:24). Jesus' disciples are living sacrifices (see Rom. 12:1), and they are to be salted or purified with the fire of trials and testings. Salt is good as long as it stays salty. Christians are to have the qualities within them that salt symbolizes, and they are to season the world with those qualities (v. 50). Jesus added that disciples are to be at peace with one another (v. 50; see 9:34 for a possible connection with this thought).

Two streams of thought have intermingled: Jesus committed his life to give us life. Such sacrifice demands the totality of man in commitment to Christ.

The Way of Discipleship
10

Mark 8:27 to 9:50 focuses on Jesus' teaching about his messiahship and what it means to follow the Messiah. Mark 10 actually carries out the same theme, but it spells out specific details about discipleship. Every incident of the passage highlights some phase of discipleship—either learning or following. Jesus even used conversation with nondisciples as an opportunity to teach his disciples. In Mark 10 Jesus seems to turn on one light after another until he has illuminated the full meaning of discipleship.

Mark 9 formally ended Jesus' Galilean ministry. Mark 10—15 records the Judean ministry. However, from the turning point of Mark 8:27 onward, there is a sense in which only the name Jerusalem is really important. Everything would come to a climax in Jerusalem.

Ideals—Not Ideas (10:1–12)

Once again Jesus was surrounded by crowds; and, as usual, he taught them. The know-it-all Pharisees who came to Jesus were just the opposite of learners. They had come not to get knowledge from Jesus, but to trap him with the question: "Is it lawful for a man to divorce his wife?" (Mark 10:2). Some writers have pointed out that the Pharisees may have hoped Jesus would suffer the fate of John the Baptist, who had lost his head when he taught God's will and refused to compromise on this matter (see Mark 6:14–29).

Of course, any answer Jesus gave would have put him in conflict with one of the pharisaic ideas about divorce (see Matt. 19:1–9). As the parallel account in Matthew reveals, the basic question was not whether divorce was permitted but for what reasons it might be permitted. Deuteronomy 24:1 was generally accepted as a statement of legal procedure for divorce, but there were two rabbinic schools that held opposite and extreme views on reasons for divorce. The school of Hillel believed that a man could divorce his wife for almost any reason: spoiling the food, dancing in the streets, talking with a strange man, letting her husband hear her speak disrespectfully about her in-laws, being a loudmouthed brawling woman. One rabbi even extended the reason for divorce as being adequate if the husband should find someone he liked better than his wife. The school of Shammai gave adultery as the only reason for divorce. Which of the two schools do you think was more popular with the men of the day?

Jesus altered the question and turned it back to the Pharisees (v. 3). Jesus asked them what Moses had *commanded*. The Pharisees answered quickly and correctly that Moses had *permitted* divorce—he had not commanded it. But perhaps they missed the subtlety between *commanded* and *permitted*. Moses was a lawgiver; he did not make a moral pronouncement on divorce in Deuteronomy 24:1. So Jesus began his teaching by telling why Moses had given such instructions about divorce. Since stony hearts had forced the matter of divorce, Moses had given a commandment of legal requirements as a concession and not as a condonement of divorce. Exodus 20:14 was God's commandment, and the legal process for divorce did not make God's commandment and intentions void (see Mark 10:10–12).

Jesus pulled apart the pharisaic dilemma about reasons for divorce by showing that God intended for a man and woman to marry, leave their parents, become one, and discipline themselves to live together for life. Jesus was not a lawgiver to talk about minimums; he was a bestower of grace to tell about God's will and the maximum results of living by it. Therefore, while the Pharisees held legalistic ideas about divorce, Jesus taught God's ideal that could be real in marriage. The religious leaders had asked Jesus what was legal, but he answered with what was right according to God's intentions (see Gen. 1:27; 2:24).

Habitually, Pharisees asked questions in public to trap Jesus. The disciples usually kept quiet while he was teaching in public, but later in private they would ask questions to learn and to get clarification. They continued that pattern in this instance (v. 10), and Jesus rewarded the questioners with fresh insights. Jesus taught that a wife had equal status and equal responsibility with the husband in matters of marriage and divorce. This teaching was new from a Jewish perspective.

According to Jewish law, a man could not be charged with adultery against his own wife, but she could be charged with adultery against her husband (see Deut. 22:13–30). (However, the husband could be charged with adultery against another man's wife.) In Roman law a woman could divorce her husband, but in Jewish law a woman could not divorce her husband, technically speaking. In Jewish law the act of divorce remained as the husband's act, but the wife could claim various reasons as justification for divorce. Some examples are: denial of sexual rights, impotence, leprosy, entrance into a disgusting trade, and other select reasons. In Jewish law the woman was discriminated against.

Jesus simply pointed out that the person who divorces or deserts his mate and marries another commits adultery (vv. 11–12). He made no distinction between husband and wife, male and female. So Jesus elevated the status of woman to that of man's, regardless of what Jewish law had taught. A man could be guilty of adultery against his own wife just as a wife could be guilty of adultery against her husband. Jesus' point was that a legal act of man does not do away with the spiritual effect of broken oneness that occurs by divorce and remarriage. The ideal would be broken. Jesus did not deal with opinion and circumstances.

While divorce is not the unpardonable sin, it breaks God's intentions for two people who have become one in marriage. What about circumstances? Jesus was teaching the kingdom of God—God's intended will. It was no time to go into endless circumstances. When God's ideal will is not done in a life, he continues to will what is best under the circumstances for that life. No one was ever more understanding and forgiving than Jesus. But he gave us the way of discipleship in marriage as a positive teaching. God's way in marriage is the right way.

Essential Qualities of Discipleship (10:13–16)

The disciples tried to guard Jesus' privacy time and again, but Jesus never refused to see anyone. In fact, it bothered Jesus that the disciples tried to stop the seemingly unimportant children from coming to Jesus for the blessing of his touch. So Jesus took the children in his arms and blessed them. In the midst of this warm scene, Jesus taught an object lesson about kingdom citizenship (which includes discipleship). The Jewish children did not depict a sentimental scene of innocence (as some have thought); rather, the children portrayed trust, humility, and obedience. They were completely dependent upon their parents. It is the childlike quality of complete dependence that every true disciple must have. Jesus' disciples are to be characterized by dependence, humility, obedience, and willingness to let God give them citizenship into his kingdom as a gift of grace. These qualities are essential to discipleship.

One Way to Discipleship (10:17–22)

Of all the sad people who came to Jesus, only one man is said to have gone away sad: That man was the rich young ruler (Mark 10:22; Matt. 19:22; Luke 18:23). How the would-be disciple became grieved is a tender and tragic story.

With all the enthusiasm of youth, the wealthy ruler ran to Jesus to ask what he could do to inherit eternal life. (Had he inherited his possessions?) Perhaps he unthinkingly blurted out the title "Good Teacher" (as Jesus' rebuke in v. 18 would indicate); nevertheless, the man showed his sincerity by kneeling. He wanted eternal life, and he wrongly thought that he could do something to inherit it.

Jesus patiently interviewed the man and then brought him to the crossroads of decision about discipleship. With that divine power of analysis, Jesus realized the candidate for discipleship knew and lived the second part of the Ten Commandments: the ones dealing with man's relationship to man. Sure enough, the young man replied that he had kept all those commandments since he was a boy (v. 20).

Jesus felt a deep love for the likable inquirer, but that love did not keep the climax from coming rapidly. First, Jesus told the rich young ruler that he still lacked one thing. Then, to the man who was used to giving orders, Jesus gave five staccato-like commands: Go, sell, give, come, and follow me (v. 21). The ruler's spirits collapsed, for his lack was related to what he had the most of: possessions. He would not surrender all of self and possessions to follow Jesus. In despair, the man who had rejected Jesus and eternal life walked away from discipleship with his very temporary possessions of wealth, youth, and power.

Discipleship is a one-way road that the rich young ruler refused to travel. By definition, he could not be a disciple: "Only the man who says goodbye to all his possessions can be my disciple" (Luke 14:33, Phillips). To become a disciple of Jesus means to start life over again; and the rich young ruler was not willing to become a child spiritually. He was not willing to deny himself what he had that stood between him and Jesus. Other rich people may follow Jesus, keep their money, and use it for him. The point is that the way of discipleship calls for a person to rid himself of anything that stands between him and Jesus.

Absolute Grace (10:23–27)

After the rich young ruler went away, Jesus commented to his disciples that it would be hard for the wealthy to enter the kingdom of God. The disciples were amazed. Jesus added that it would be hard for anyone to enter the kingdom of God (v. 24; note the difference between the RSV and KJV renderings). And the disciples were dumbfounded when Jesus used an impossible comparison to tell how hard— or impossible—it would be for a rich man to enter the kingdom of God (vv. 25–26).

To understand the disciples' keen amazement at Jesus' warning about wealth, we must realize that the Jewish people equated wealth with the special favor of God. If a wealthy man could not enter the kingdom of God easier than a camel going through the eye of a needle, then the disciples wanted to know who on earth could be expected to enter. "The eye of a needle" must be taken literally in verse 25. Theologian A. M. Hunter has said: "There is no evidence for the widely current view that a small gate in Jerusalem bore the name 'Needle's Eye.' That gate exists . . . only in the imagination of Jerusalem guides! The figure of the camel and the needle's eye is a picturesque hyperbole for the well-nigh impossible."[1] The camel was the largest animal that came to mind, and the needle's eye was the smallest opening. However, twice in the Talmud (Jewish writings), there is reference to the impossibility of an elephant's passing through the eye of a needle. In the picturesque language of the Hebrews, impossible comparisons were used to make a point. What point was Jesus making?

Jesus had pointed out how hard it would be for rich people and others to enter the kingdom of God. And with the impossible comparison, Jesus, in effect, answered that salvation is possible only by the grace of God. We will do well to notice that Jesus called his disciples "children" in verse 24. They had that absolute dependence that opens the door for God's absolute grace. God gives what neither money nor merit can buy.

Dividends of Discipleship (10:28–31)

When Peter told Jesus that he and the other disciples had left all to follow Jesus, Peter implied a question: "We have done all that you commanded the rich young ruler to do for eternal life; now what are we going to get in return?" Jesus answered Peter with three prophetic promises: (1) one hundred times as much as a disciple gives up for the sake of Christ and the gospel, (2) the challenge of persecutions, and (3) the fulfillment of eternal life—which has already begun for those who trust Jesus. The statement in verse 31 reassured the disciples that final judgment lay with God. His judgment will reverse the order of some judgments and priorities that man makes.

The price and the promise of discipleship were interwoven in Jesus' statement. The only qualification for receiving the promises was proper motivation on the part of disciples ("for my sake and for the gospel," v. 29).

Disciples unto Death (10:32–34)

Jesus walked toward his death while his disciples followed him. It was customary for a teacher to walk ahead of his disciples, but more was involved here than custom. The atmosphere hung heavy with the disciples' dread about Jesus' direction and what that meant for him and them. The disciples' emotions showed something of the price they voluntarily paid to be Jesus' disciples. They were dismayed and afraid. They followed a man on his way to death, and they did not understand all of his teachings. Still they followed him! (Scholars differ on whether one group or two groups followed Jesus—v. 32. Either way, the twelve disciples were Jesus' primary focus at this time.)

Jesus and his disciples were going to Jerusalem. People had come from Jerusalem to hear John the Baptist and be baptized by him (1:5). They had come from Jerusalem to Jesus because of what they had heard about him (3:8). Scribes had come from Jerusalem to denounce Jesus' authority and to attack him and his disciples (3:22; 7:1). Now Jesus was going to Jerusalem (10:32–33). Jesus had begun his Father's business in his Father's house in Jerusalem, and he was on his way to complete that business (Luke 2:49). Though the direction to Jerusalem was down by the map, some things are more important than geography. Jerusalem was the holy city that set òn a hill, and that made the direction up from wherever a Jew was traveling.

Jesus paused to give his disciples a third major prophecy about his approaching death and resurrection. Each of the three prophecies included the promise of resurrection on the third day (8:31; 9:31; 10:33–34). But the facts of death grew more vivid with each prophecy: first, an announcement; then an implication of betrayal; and now the details of trial, mockery, and scourging appeared. We can see this increasing vividness in prophecy in chart form:*

Events Prophesied About Christ	Mark 8:31	Mark 9:31	Mark 10:33–34	Suffering Narrative
1. Betrayed/delivered to chief priests and scribes	—	✓	✓	14:53
2. Rejected/condemned by chief priests and scribes	✓	—	✓	14:64
3. Handed over to Romans (Gentiles)	—	—	✓	15:1
4. Humiliated and beaten	—	—	✓	14:65; 15:15–20
5. Executed	✓	✓	✓	15:24
6. Resurrected	✓	✓	✓	16:1–8

The disciples seemed to love and trust Jesus so much that they followed him even when they could not understand everything he told them. Almost to a person, they would be disciples to both Jesus' death and theirs.

Standards for Greatness (10:35–45)

There are a lot of standards for judging greatness, but there are two standards that stand in stark contrast to each other.

Worldly standards (vv. 35–40).—In spite of all Jesus' teachings, James and John still had worldly dreams of occupying the highest positions in Jesus' kingdom. They and their mother still misunderstood the nature of the kingdom of God (see Matt. 20:20–21; but also see Matt. 27:56). "Right hand" and "left hand" were Jewish terms for being next to the king in honor. Jesus graciously told the disciples that they did not know what they were asking. In fact, if Jesus had literally fulfilled James and John's request, they would have occupied the other two crosses on Golgotha; for it was on Golgotha that Christ was exalted—lifted up, then glorified by the Father.

---

* This chart is adapted from commentaries by Vincent Taylor and William L. Lane (see the bibliography for publication information).

When Jesus asked James and John if they could drink of his cup and be baptized with his baptism, he phrased the question in such a way that implied he expected an answer of no. But they simultaneously answered yes. Little did they realize that "cup" and "baptism"—the age-old symbols for suffering—meant death on a cross. Nevertheless, Jesus agreed with the disciples' answer; for he foresaw an early martyr's death for James (Acts 12:2) and a long living martyrdom for John. Yet Jesus had to add that the places of honor were not for him to give. That choice belonged to his heavenly Father.

Heavenly standards (vv. 41–45).—When the other disciples learned what James and John had been up to, they got mad. But Jesus stopped the talk and contrasted worldly standards with heavenly standards. Very simply, the Gentiles (literally, "nations") judged a person's greatness by how many people he had under his authority. Jesus told his disciples that the Gentile way was not the way to greatness.

In contrast, Jesus said, two things characterize the heavenly way to greatness. First, whoever wants to be great has to be a servant (v. 43). Next, whoever wants to be the greatest of all has to be the slave of all (v. 44). Then Jesus used his messianic title (Son of man) in saying that he himself had come to serve and not to be served.

Then, for the first time in the book of Mark, Jesus interpreted the purpose of his life. He came to die in our place (v. 45). He came as a ransom to free those who were kidnapped by sin. This word for ransom is used only here and in Matthew 20:28 in the New Testament. But related words that talk about ransom, redeem, or redemption appear in a number of places (see Luke 1:68; 2:38; 24:21; Titus 2:14; Heb. 9:12; 1 Pet. 1:18). The text does not press the terminology to say who receives the ransom; nor should that be as important as the deliverance of captives by the life of Christ (see Isa. 53:10–12 for the fact of Christ's death taking the place of sinful man).

So Jesus not only told the price of discipleship; he lived out discipleship for others to see as he followed the will of God.

Sight and Discipleship (10:46–52)

When Jesus passed blind Bartimaeus, Bartimaeus knew that Jesus was his only hope for sight and an end to begging. So he frantically called Jesus by the messianic title "Son of David"; and he begged Jesus to have mercy on him. Jesus stopped and ordered the man brought to him—despite the attempts of the people to silence Bartimaeus and let Jesus go on. Then with Bartimaeus before him, Jesus asked: "What do you want me to do for you?" (v. 51). James and John were asked that same question by Jesus (v. 36). They had wanted position. Bartimaeus needed sight, and Jesus gave Bartimaeus what he needed. Now Bartimaeus may have had good days in begging for money; but that day he did the best bit of begging in all his life, for Jesus announced that Bartimaeus' faith had made him well. Immediately he could see, and he used his sight to follow Jesus (v. 52). Need, gratitude, and loyalty sum up the story of Bartimaeus; and they also sum up the phases of discipleship.

Note

1. A. M. Hunter, *The Gospel According to Saint Mark* (London: SCM Press, Ltd., 1949), p. 104.

Authoritative Teachings and Actions
11—12

Jesus forcefully revealed his messiahship through authoritative teachings and actions. From this point on the events occurred in and around Jerusalem. There were quiet times, but there were also times of stormy conflict. In one scene after another, Jesus emerged as the undisputed Master Teacher; but in every clash with the Jewish leaders, Jesus came one step closer to the cross.

Authority Acclaimed (11:1–11)

Jesus and his disciples came from Jericho to the suburbs of Jerusalem. Bethphage, Bethany, and the Mount of Olives were all within two miles of Jerusalem (see John 11:18). It was Passover time, when the Jewish great expectations for messianic deliverance were at their highest (see Ex. 11—13; Lev. 23:5–8). Exact time pegs for this last week of Jesus' earthly ministry are not certain as we compare the four Gospels, but the events and their meanings acclaim Jesus' authority.

The messianic secret came to an end when Jesus entered Jerusalem on what is now referred to as Palm Sunday. Until then Jesus had not publicly revealed his messiahship except through veiled action. Now he deliberately and purposefully chose to reveal his messiahship with a symbol more meaningful than words could ever be. He rode into Jerusalem on a donkey (see Zech. 9:9; Matt. 21:4–5; John 12:14–16). The fact that the donkey had never been ridden gave something of a symbolic sacredness to Jesus' use of it. The crowds received Jesus as the Messiah. The two disciples had spread their garments on the donkey in place of a saddle. The crowds had spread their outer garments and leafy branches in the road. Then ahead of Jesus and behind him the people shouted, "Hosanna! Blessed be he who comes in the name of the Lord! Blessed is the kingdom of our father David that is coming! Hosanna in the highest!" (Mark 11:9–10). *Hosanna* is a Hebrew word that means "Save, we pray!" (See Ps. 118:25–26.)

Contrary to the crowd's earthly hopes, Jesus had come without arms and without an army. He was a king of peace who had arrived on a symbol of peace—a donkey. To Jewish people, peace means more than absence of conflict; it means having God's highest blessing. As Jesus came to lead a spiritual rebellion against wrong, he offered those who would trust him the potential for peace in its fullest meaning.

Interpreters differ on several points in Mark 11:1–10. They question whether *Lord* (v. 3) refers to Jesus or to the owner of the donkey. Though no one can be sure, the reference seems to be to Jesus himself. Otherwise, why would the disciples need to tell anyone that the owner would send the donkey back immediately? (v. 3). While Jesus knew that he was fulfilling prophecy with his triumphal entry into Jerusalem, how much did the people know? Their praise of Jesus seemed to be spontaneous; but even with their cry of hosanna, there is some question about how much they understood (see John 12:16 for a comment about the disciples' understanding). The depth of understanding for Jesus and the crowds surely was different. But it seems that the crowd acclaimed Jesus for who he was: the Messiah.

After Jesus surveyed the desecration of the Temple, he went back to Bethany. The Bible implies that Jesus waited to exercise his rightful authority in cleansing the Temple because it was too late on that particular day (v. 11). For a time, the pattern was Jerusalem by day and Bethany by night. And at the end of the day, we can sense that it was the quiet before the storm.

Purposeful Power (11:12–14)

On the way to Jerusalem from Bethany, Jesus got hungry; and he saw a fig tree leafed out with the promise of fruit. But when Jesus got to the fig tree, he found it barren. With a word Jesus withered the tree. The mysterious event may be taken literally or symbolically as a parable.

Literally, the incident shows that uselessness invites disaster; further, the incident condemns hypocrisy. Taken symbolically, the fig tree incident stands for Israel's unfruitfulness and approaching doom. Either way, Jesus used his power to teach a solemn and important lesson. In Jesus' other miracles, he blessed or healed; but in this instance Jesus prophesied condemnation: either of hypocritical and unfruitful individuals or of the barren nation of Israel.

Students of the Bible are puzzled over the fact that Jesus gave a death sentence to the fig tree when it was not yet the fig season. Interpreters have to have an answer for everything, or they tend to want to delete what they can't understand. And there are those who feel that "it was not the season for figs" (v. 13) was not originally in the Gospel of Mark. They think some scribe added it at a later time. The clause is not in the parallel verse of Matthew 21:19, but there is no textual reason to dismiss the statement from Mark.

The time was the middle of April, and figs normally did not ripen until June. So some students believe that although Jesus was hungry he did not expect to find fruit on the fig tree. He wanted to use the incident to teach his disciples a lesson about Israel. However, Jesus was hungry, and there was the chance that there might be some early green figs on the tree. Notice this thought in verse 13: "He went to see if he could find *anything* on it." (Italics added.) The details are not as important as the context of the miracle. Notice what follows (also see Mic. 7:1–6; Jer. 8:13; Luke 13:6–9).

Authoritative Action (11:15–19)

When Jesus got to the Temple in Jerusalem, he found it as barren of spiritual fruit as the fig tree had been of figs. He had been in the Temple the evening before, and things had not changed in the meantime. The holy Temple had become an unholy cattle market where worshipers were cheated out of their money. Worshipers had to exchange their money (Greek, Roman, or whatever) for the Jewish money that had to be used to pay dues in the Temple. Naive souls were at the mercy of crooked money changers. Pilgrims came with money but without sacrifices, so they bought those when they got to the Temple. Business people were using the Temple courts as a thoroughfare. Besides the desecration, the merchants had stolen the court of the Gentiles, which was the only place those of other nations could pray and worship. (*Nations* in v. 17 and *Gentiles* translate the same Greek word.)

With explosive force Jesus ended it all! His authoritative action, coupled with prophetic truth (Isa. 56:7; Jer. 7:11), amazed the scribes and chief priests and struck fear in them. Jesus' attack was sudden, but it was not hit-and-run. He stayed and would not allow anyone to carry anything through the Temple (v. 16). In fact, he and his disciples didn't leave until evening (v. 19); so they were probably there several hours.

Jesus had challenged the authority and pocketbooks of the conniving scribes and chief priests. They were afraid they would lose their following, so they could hardly wait to destroy Jesus (v. 18). The scribes and chief priests might have had more fear and might have changed their plans if they had been with Jesus on his way to the Temple and on the next morning.

Access to Authority (11:20–26)

While Jesus and his disciples traveled from Bethany to Jerusalem, they saw a dried-up fig tree. Peter was amazed when he realized it was the tree Jesus had cursed just the day before. Of course, Jesus was not surprised; and the incident gave him an excellent opportunity to teach his disciples that power to wither a tree or to move a mountain depends on faith in God. Doubt is an obstacle that ruins the power of prayer for those who are pure in heart and right in motive as they pursue God's will. The key to answered prayer is faith, belief, trust. Jesus' point was that by faith his followers can do what seems impossible or even absurd.

Verse 25 shows that mountain-moving faith goes together with forgiving love. Prayer and resentment do not go together. The person who is unforgiving and prays for forgiveness defeats his prayer by his own attitudes and actions. Forgiveness is the bridge that the praying person has to pass over to receive his own forgiveness. So faith, a pure heart, and a right motive go together in prayers that have power and bring answers. Verse 26 is not in the best manuscripts (but see Matt. 6:15).

Stalemate (11:27–33)

A religious delegation asked Jesus for his religious credentials—his authority for cleansing the Temple. If Jesus had replied that his authority was divine, the theologians could have accused him of blasphemy (though the charge would have been wrong). However, Jesus met the opening question with a paralyzing and defeating counterquestion: Was the authority of John the Baptist from heaven or from man? Jesus' question implied that his source of authority was the same as that of John the Baptist. So Jesus forced his adversaries to answer by their own thinking.

The people had accepted John as a prophet, but the Pharisees and lawyers had not (Luke 7:29–30). So to admit that John's authority was divine would be a self-condemnation for the religious leaders; further, it would be an admission that Jesus was the Messiah. For John had claimed that Jesus was from God (see John 1:29–36). On the other hand, to deny that John's authority was from heaven would condemn the popular belief of the people. And that would never do. So the religious leaders gave the only answer left to them: "We do not know" (v. 33). They were beaten.

After such a crushing defeat, it was anticlimactic when Jesus added that he would not reveal the source of his authority (for the cleansing of the Temple and for his entire ministry may be meant). However, it was obvious that everyone—even the religious leaders—knew that the authority of John and Jesus was divine authority. The members from the Jewish court known as the Sanhedrin had questioned Jesus to trap him. The result was that, probably for the first time in their legalistic lives, they had had to say, "We do not know." Neither ignorance nor doubt was their problem; they were guilty of having knowledge and ability to decide truth and act upon it but choosing to disobey God's revealed will.

The question about Jesus' authority was the first of a series of questions to trap him. They would also question him about taxation, resurrection, and the most important commandment—after a parable of judgment.

Ultimate Authority (12:1–12)

Jesus followed the unanswered questions with a parable about the story of redemption. A man set up a business to produce wine. He provided all the equipment necessary: a wine vat to keep the juice after it was pressed, a wall to keep out animals, a tower so that the workers could keep watch and have shelter. He owned the vineyard, planted it, enlisted sharecroppers, entrusted the business to them, and left for another country. When the payday of sharing time came, the owner sent for his share. His trust was betrayed; his servant was beaten and sent away empty-handed; and the vineyard was profitless to the owner (see Isa. 5:1–7; 16:10). Each person the owner sent was either beaten or killed by the tenants. The owner sent his son, who came with the full authority of the father and should have received that respect. The tenants decided to kill the heir and claim the land as being ownerless. They had already shown that they believed "possession to be nine-tenths of the law" (as the saying goes). Situations like this one were real before and during the time of Jesus' earthly ministry. But Jesus told this parable as a judgment on his hearers.

The symbolism of the parable was this: The vineyard was Israel; the owner was God; the tenants were the Jewish leaders; the slaves (translated *servants*, RSV) were the prophets; and the son was Christ. Jesus concluded the parable by asking and then answering his own question about the ultimate fate of the tenants (v. 9). The tenants would be destroyed, and the vineyard would be entrusted to others. The destruction undoubtedly looked ahead to the destruction of Jerusalem that would occur in A.D. 70.

In verses 10–11 Jesus emphasized the religious leaders' rejection of the Messiah by quoting from Psalm 118:22–23. He had already stated the rejection in other words (vv. 6–8). The cornerstone was a key stone in holding together a building or an arch. Scholars sometimes refer to a stone that was discarded in the building of Solomon's Temple, only to be reclaimed and placed as the cornerstone later in the building. Whether that reference is intended here, we do know that the prophecy was true: The representatives from the Sanhedrin rejected Jesus, and he was and is the cornerstone of God's kingdom building (see Eph. 2:20; 1 Pet. 2:6). The people rejected God's supreme and final appeal before the destruction of Jerusalem.

This parable was one that needed no explanation. The religious leaders saw themselves in the parable as the rejecters of the Messiah, the murderers of the Messiah, and the condemned tenants. With their seething rage held in check only by their fear of the people, Jesus' opponents left (v. 12).

To Pay or Not to Pay? (12:13–17)

Although the Pharisees and Herodians were natural enemies, they had entered into an unholy alliance to trap Jesus (v. 13; see 3:6). Representatives from the Sanhedrin or other defeated opponents of Jesus must have sent the Pharisees and Herodians. Religion and politics do make strange bedfellows. The Pharisees thought of themselves as the purist representatives of God, who also represented the best interests of the Jewish people. The Herodians were a political party of Jews who supported Herod Antipas and, consequently, supported Rome. These two groups wanted to bait Jesus and catch him like a fish.

Before the adversaries of Jesus sprang their question, they flattered Jesus to try to get him to lower his defenses and to guarantee a straight answer to what seemed an ironclad dilemma—an inescapable trap. They pointed out that Jesus did not look on the face of man; he was not partial; his concern was to teach God's will (v. 14). Then they asked Jesus if it was lawful to pay taxes to Caesar. Beyond the question of legality, they asked whether they ought to pay or were permitted to pay the tribute (v. 15). *Taxes* (v. 14) translates the Greek word *census* (or poll tax). All Judea was under Rome, and everyone of adult age through retirement age had to pay the tax with one specific coin: a Roman denarius, which was a small silver coin.

The question placed Jesus between Roman law and the opinion of Jews who despised the law of paying the poll tax. If Jesus answered yes, he would be a traitor in the eyes of the people (especially in the eyes of the Zealots). If Jesus answered no, he could be branded a seditionist—guilty of treason. The unholy allies must have squirmed with smug satisfaction at the cunning of their devilish question.

Jesus knew his questioners' hypocrisy and their evil motive. Nevertheless, he asked for a tax coin. Then by asking whose image and name were on the coin, Jesus caused his questioners to tear apart their carefully built dilemma; for they had to answer "Caesar's" (v. 16). All emperors were known as Caesar, but this particular one would have been Tiberius Caesar.

In those days people held that coinage was a sign of a king's power over his conquered land. The coinage was in a sense the property of the king whose image and inscription it bore. Therefore, the bitter one-word answer of "Caesar's" contained the first part of Jesus' answer. Jesus told the people that they were to give back to Caesar what was his. God's people have earthly citizenship responsibilities.

Then Jesus added a great truth: Give back to God what is his. Man is made in the image of God, and man owes his life to God whose image he bears. Human beings are the coin of the spiritual kingdom; they bear the image of the King, and they belong to the King—God himself.

So Jesus did more than get out of the trap when he answered the question. He set forth a principle for Christian citizenship for all ages. It is God's plan for people to pay the obligations they owe their government. This teaching did not condone the tax coin's claim that Caesar was divine; nor did it condone all that the Roman government did. (See Acts 5:29 for balance about a person's behavior when government conflicts with God's will.) Jesus' reply left his questioners speechless and baffled.

Two Different Worlds (12:18–27)

The Sadducees were a one-world people who did not believe in the resurrection. It is hard to be dogmatic about all that the Sadducees believed and who made up the sect because they disappeared from the scene after the destruction of Jerusalem in A.D. 70 and left little direct evidence. However, traditionally, the Sadducees were priests of the Temple and came from aristocratic families of Jerusalem. We do know that the Sadducees looked to the first five books of the Bible (the Pentateuch) for their doctrinal beliefs and that they did not believe in resurrection from the dead, angels, demons, spirits, or Jesus (see Acts 23:8). The Pharisees did believe in the resurrection from the dead, angels, demons, and spirits.

The Sadducees' example of seven brothers, one wife, and no children stemmed from what was called levirate marriage (Deut. 25:5–10; Ruth 4:5; Mark 12:19–22). (A levir is a brother-in-law.) If a brother died without any children, it was the duty of his brother to take the widow as his wife; then the first son from this union was to be registered as the son of the dead brother. This plan would continue the name of the dead brother, build up his house, and secure the inheritance of family property.

Although the example the Sadducees chose is looked upon as far-fetched and absurd, the ancient but nonbiblical book of Tobit tells about a woman who was married to seven husbands who died childless (they were slain on their wedding night). Whatever the origin of the example, the Sadducees used it to question Jesus and ridicule belief in the resurrection (v. 23). They intended to put down Jesus as a teacher and to imply that life beyond the grave would have to include polygamy (see v. 19 for the lofty title of *teacher* they had bestowed on Jesus with the intention of undermining him).

Jesus told the Sadducees they were wrong on two counts: They knew neither the Scriptures nor the power of God (v. 24). They based their doctrinal stance on the first five books of the Bible, but they had an incomplete understanding of even those books. In their mind they had limited God by what they could understand; and they had misunderstood. They had assumed that resurrection and heaven had to be a repetition of things as they are on earth. They did not recognize the power of God to overcome death with the gift of life and to create a new order that would be bigger and better than the one on earth. The Sadducees considered themselves specialists in biblical interpretation, so Jesus' charge of wrongness on these two counts must have stung.

Jesus went on to teach that in the world to come man would have angel-like perfect communion with God, and there would be no marriage. The Bible does not say that we will become angels; nor does it say that we will not know our mates in life after death. Jesus was using earthly language to tell the Sadducees that the coming order will be different from the present order (v. 25).

Jesus used Exodus 3:6 to illustrate that the deceased patriarchs were with God and that God is the God of the living (vv. 26–27). He who provides salvation and deliverance during life does not stop that provision at death; he raises us from death. Jesus based the promise of resurrection on the power of God. And, as he had begun, he told the Sadducees they were very wrong.

Authority and Priority (12:28–34)

Jesus' superb response to the Sadducees impressed a scribe and led the scribe to ask a question. He wanted to know which commandment had priority over all others (v. 28). Since the rabbis had listed 613 different commandments (248 affirmative and 365 negative), the question was a natural one.

Jesus met the sincere question with a straightforward answer. He called attention to the uniqueness and oneness of God as the foundation for saying that loving God completely is the first commandment. Then Jesus gave more than he was asked: He taught that love for one's neighbor is the commandment that is second in priority. It did not take a lawyer to understand Jesus' interpretation of the Law. The indivisible truth was that when a person gives God his first love, he will also love his neighbor. Jesus had put together the truths of Deuteronomy 6:4–5 and Leviticus 19:18. The portion from Deuteronomy was the beginning of the *Shema* (meaning *hear* from the first word of the verse); and every Jew recited the *Shema* every day. The call to love God with heart, soul, mind, and strength was a call for total love and complete expression of that love. There was no attempt to divide man into parts.

Love for others arises out of our love for God. Leviticus 19:18 referred to loving a fellow Israelite when it referred to neighbor. But when Jesus referred to neighbor in Mark 12:31, he meant that we are to love anyone in need (see Luke 10:29–37). Nationality and location do not exempt anyone from being our neighbor.

The scribe agreed with Jesus and called him by the title *teacher.* Then the scribe repeated what Jesus had taught but added that the recognition of God's uniqueness and the expression of love were more important than offerings and sacrifices (Mark 12:32–33). When any person accepts the sovereignty of God and the authority of Jesus, he can know that he is near the kingdom of God. Jesus commended the scribe and implied that he needed to make a further commitment based on what he believed (v. 34). Jesus had defeated all trap questions, and he had answered the scribe's sincere question.

Sonship and Lordship (12:35–44)

Jesus did not wait for questions to continue his teaching. He went to the Temple, asked questions that needed to be answered, and provoked thought.

It was well known that the Messiah ("Christ," v. 35) would be a descendant of David. So Jesus referred to Psalm 110:1 (a Davidic psalm) and in essence asked: "How could David call his own son his lord?" If the answer had come, it would have been phrased something like this: The Messiah was to be David's son as a descendant by birth, but David's lord by divine nature. This Holy-Spirit-inspired truth called for a realization that the Messiah was much more than a mere human descendant of David. There were no glazed-over eyes as Jesus taught. The people were alive with attention and glad to be stimulated by such thought-provoking questions.

Misused Authority (12:38–40)

To the average Jew, the scribes were people of authority, for they were experts at explaining the law of Moses. But Jesus cautioned the people against following so-called experts when they misuse their authority by calling attention to it. The scribes' egotism and selfishness expressed itself through the clothes they wore, the greetings they expected in public, the choice seats in synagogue and at feasts, the widows' money they wasted, and long prayers that lacked genuineness. The long, white scholarly robes contrasted with the colorful clothes of the common people. In public the people greeted scribes by bowing and by recognizing their authority through a title such as rabbi or master. At church the scribes wanted to sit and be seen at the front. At feasts they wanted the place of honor next to the host. Their services were supposed to be free, but the offerings that supported them also opened the door to abuse. In some way the scribes were devouring (swallowing or eating up) widows' property. Were the scribes' long prayers for the widows? And if so, were the prayers only a long, hypocritical exercise to get more money? Or perhaps the scribes had other ways of devouring the widows' property and then prayed long prayers to cover up the kind of men they were.

Jesus did not condemn all religious leaders, but he did condemn those who were guilty of hypocrisy, self-righteousness, and covetousness. Their self-centered attitudes led them to misuse authority. The need for Jesus' caution did not end with those who heard him that day. The warning still applies. And those who fail to be good stewards of their positions face greater condemnation than the less privileged.

Spiritual Scales (12:41–44)

Jesus used the action of a widow to picture true giving. He sat where he could see a widow put two mites into the Temple treasury. A mite was the smallest coin in circulation; two of them were worth less than a penny (since a mite was about one-eighth of a cent normally). She could have kept one or both of the mites, but she gave all she had. Her meager amount was contrasted by the large offerings the rich people had given before her. Her two mites would have seemed small even against the pocket change the crowd gave. It would have been humiliating if the giver had to call out the amount of the offering as some interpreters think. However, Mark records that Jesus was where he could see and does not mention what he heard. Either way, it was the widow who went away with the special blessing and notice of Jesus. He pointed out that the widow had given what was essential to her life; the others had given out of their over-flow. On spiritual scales, the greatest gift is that which costs the giver the most.

As far as we know, Jesus never returned to the Temple again. He knew that judgment was coming upon Jerusalem and the Temple.

Facing the Future
13

Mark 13 is an assurance chapter punctuated with commands on how to face the future. Specific interpretations are often difficult, however; and though theologians all have their viewpoints, few are dogmatic about their interpretations. The writing is prophecy that is steeped in Jewish thought and terminology about the Day of the Lord. In fact, scholars refer to Mark 13 as "The Little Apocalypse" (meaning "The Little Revelation"). In other words, the purpose of Mark 13 is to provide Jesus' followers with enlightenment to live by, not obscure teachings that cause anxiety.

Language has its limitations. When language cannot communicate adequately in a literal way, the language necessarily becomes picture language. The language of revelation (apocalyptic language) is picto-rial, and it envisions the future rather than recording history. How-ever, the picture language is rooted in Jewish history and ideas. So we have imagery from the past and teachings about the future.

We have to see Mark 13 against three future events: (1) the death of Jesus, (2) the destruction of the Temple and Jerusalem, and (3) the Day of the Lord—when Christ would return and time would end. We would like to know many more details about people, time, and places indicated in Mark 13; but we would do well to focus on the clarity of the big picture instead of pressing on matters that no one knows for sure. The biggest problem seems to be in deciding what passages refer to the destruction of Jerusalem and what passages refer to the second coming of Christ. We will deal with that problem. But, again, the certainties of the chapter outweigh the uncertainties; and Jesus' instructions are clear for every age. We can see these truths in summary form and then pause to consider more understanding of the various sections (see the parallels in Matthew 24—25; Luke 21:5–36).

Jesus prophesied Jerusalem's destruction. That prophecy was fulfilled in A.D. 70 when Rome smashed Jerusalem and its magnificent Temple. Further, Jesus boldly told his disciples to face and to endure the persecution that was certain to come after his death. He warned about false messiahs. Interspersed with the other prophecies was Jesus' warning about the second coming; and the final part of the chapter concludes with a warning to watch for the fulfillment of Jesus' prophecy—especially the prophecy of the second coming.

If Mark wrote his Gospel about A.D. 65, he wrote in the middle of a chaotic decade. Christians in Rome were having to deal with Nero and his persecution of them; Christians in Jerusalem faced the turmoil that would come from A.D. 66–70. The disciples Jesus spoke to had concern about the future; the first readers of Mark's Gospel had concern about the future; and we have concern about the future. The good news is that the future is secure in Jesus Christ and that he tells us how to face the future as we live in the present. So Mark 13 is a call to practical faith and not just a battleground for competing views of interpreters.

The Beginning of the End for Jerusalem (13:1–2)

As Jesus and his disciples came out of the Temple, his disciples commented on the grandeur of the Temple complex. Such a comment might seem strange since Jesus and the disciples were familiar with the Temple. It helps to know that the Temple complex was new and still being built.

For almost a thousand years, the Temple site in Jerusalem had been a place of religious importance for all Jews. Solomon's Temple was the first one. It was built about 960–950 B.C. The Babylonians destroyed that Temple in 587 B.C. Zerubbabel led in the building of a second Temple on the same site, and it was completed about 515 B.C. The second Temple was not so bad despite what writers have written about it. In fact, that Temple stood for almost five hundred years, which was longer than Solomon's Temple and Herod's Temple put together. But by comparison with Solomon's Temple and Herod's Temple, Zerubbabel's Temple came in third place.

Antiochus Epiphanes desecrated the second Temple in the second century B.C. After the desecration, the structure stood until Herod built a third Temple on the same site; and that Temple had a magnificence to match a rebuilt Jerusalem. The rabbis didn't care for Herod, but they were a regular chamber of commerce for the Temple he built. The Temple sanctuary itself was completed in about eighteen months of 20–19 B.C. But the Temple area, which included other buildings and grounds, was being enlarged to include about one-sixth of old Jerusalem (or to include an area of about thirty-five acres). This building was still going on when Jesus spoke, and it was not completed when the destruction came in A.D. 70. Some of the stones were twelve feet high, eighteen feet wide, and forty feet long. No wonder the disciples were awed by what they saw.

But the holy place of the Temple had become unholy, for it had become a den of thieves and a place of resistance against Jesus (see Mark 11:15–18). Despite that fact, the disciples were amazed at the size of the stones and the splendor of the buildings. The solid structures must have looked as if they would last for another thousand years, but in about forty years the Temple would be leveled. Jesus prophesied total destruction. And that's what happened. Fire came first; then Titus ordered the Temple destroyed. The Roman destruction of Jerusalem came as a reaction to political and military rebellion, but it was also God's judgment upon the spiritual rebellion of the Jews (see Mal. 3:1–6). Jesus announced this startling prophecy to his disciples, but he didn't include the details.

Thinking in the Future Tense (13:3–8)

The next scene is on the Mount of Olives, across from the Temple. The Temple was on a hill that was 2,470 feet above sea level. The Temple faced the east where the sun rose over Mount Olive, which was 200 feet higher than the Temple hill. From that vantage point, the original four disciples (Peter, James, John, and Andrew—1:16–20) were with Jesus, who was seated in a customary teaching position.

Jesus' prophecy had caused the disciples to start thinking in the future tense. They wanted to know when *these things* ("this," v. 4, RSV) would occur and what signs to watch for. (See vv. 23,29–30 for references to *all things* or *these things.)* The disciples referred to the prophecy about the Temple, but Jesus answered far more inclusively with his longest continuous teaching in Mark. In the rest of the chapter, he taught about two periods: specifically, about the time between the present and the destruction of Jerusalem; generally, about the time between the present and Jesus' second coming. Verses 5–8 seem to be a mixture of both the specific and the general.

Jesus was not as concerned about pinpointing time as he was about encouraging his disciples to persist in faithfulness until the end (v. 5). He did not want his disciples to be led astray by false messiahs who would claim Jesus' title and authority (v. 6). "In my name" (v. 6) would represent the authority of Christ and "I am *he"* (v. 6) would represent a claim to be Christ. They would not claim to be the personal Jesus, who is the Messiah; they would set themselves up as the Messiah. *Christ* is the Greek word and *Messiah* is the Hebrew word for God's Anointed One. (See the commentary note on Mark 6:50 for "I am *he."*) Every age seems to have its false messiahs, and the first century A.D. was no exception.

Wars, earthquakes, and famines could have referred to the recent history and the current setting of Mark's first readers. It was a time of conflict. There had been earthquakes in Laodicea (A.D. 61) and in Pompeii (A.D. 62). Judea had experienced famine in A.D. 46, and there had been other recent famines. These events would have been future tense for the disciples who were listening to Jesus; and events like them would be future tense for readers of Mark. But whatever the date on the calendar, Jesus' teachings about such events would be the same: Don't be distressed. These events are not the end itself; rather, they are the labor pains that have to come before the birth of the messianic era (vv. 7–8).

The Hard Way of Discipleship (13:9–13)

Verses 9–13 ought to be enough to end easy invitations to discipleship that fail to indicate the cost. In these verses Jesus showed an intense concern by the repeated use of *you.* He wanted his disciples to know what the future held and how to face it.

Much after the pattern of Jesus, his disciples would face judgment in courts (local sanhedrins) and beatings in synagogues and would represent Jesus in giving testimony before authorities (v. 9). The testimony would be a witness of good news; but rejected good news stands as evidence against those who refuse the testimony. (The root of the Greek word translated *testimony* has come over into English as our word for *martyr.*)

The reference in verse 9 to governors and kings may have led to the parenthesis of verse 10. The thought of Gentile authorities would call to mind the need for the good news to be preached to all nations *(nations* and *Gentiles* translate the same Greek word). *Must* (v. 10) refers to a divine necessity (also see Matt. 24:14). God alone determines the end of time, but he does give us insights to certain sequences of events.

Verse 11 pictures a court scene. In so many words, Jesus told his disciples that there was no need to anxiously practice their speeches for court testimony. They could say what came to mind because it would be from the Holy Spirit.

Christians were hated for several reasons. They were more committed to Christ than to family members or anyone else. They were misunderstood in what they believed and in how they behaved. Jesus prophesied that disciples' family members would betray them and, in some instances, cause them to be put to death. Everywhere they turned they would face hatred because of their commitment to Christ. Such hatred could tempt anyone to turn from his beliefs and desert the one he followed. But those who are faithful in discipleship even when it involves the martyrdom of death will receive eternal deliverance. A characteristic of true disciples is that they endure whatever persecution comes their way, and they do not abandon their faithful following of Christ. Not every Christian experiences the kind of persecution Jesus outlined to the disciples who listened to him, but every Christian should consider the possibility of that kind of cost when he decides to follow Jesus. Further, faithful Christian living often brings persecution of a more subtle nature. But the joy of discipleship is always worth the cost.

Hope Before the Ruins (13:14–23)

Jesus specifically answered the question of verse 4 in verses 14–23. He shared the sign that would appear before Jerusalem's destruction, and he offered hope of escape for those who would recognize

the sign and get out of Judea. These events would occur between
A.D. 66–70.

Verse 14 is the crucial verse in this passage because it describes
the "desolating sacrilege" that would signal the time to flee Jerusalem
of Judea. The King James Version translates the phrase with "abomination of desolation." The background for this terminology comes from
Daniel 9:27; 11:31; 12:11. Matthew 24:15 and Luke 21:20 are the
parallel passages.

The readers were called to pay attention and understand this prophecy. We know that Christians of the Jerusalem church did understand
because they fled north across the Jordan River to Pella of Decapolis.
But commentators differ in their understanding of what they read
in Mark 13:14. Did the abomination refer to a person or a thing?
Technically, the language of Mark would allow either interpretation
(though some insist that Mark's use of a masculine participle has to
mean that the abomination was a person). The translators of the Revised Standard Version chose to refer to the abomination as *it* rather
than *he.* (See Matt. 24:15.)

The abomination could have referred to a person who would dese-
crate the Temple as Antiochus Epiphanes had done in 168 B.C. He
had set up an altar to Zeus in the Temple, sacrificed swine that were
ceremonially unclean, and outlawed Judaism. An abomination like
that causes worshipers to leave the Temple desolate. Commentators
guess at persons from Caligula to the Antichrist to Phanni (a Zealot-
named priest) as they try to pinpoint the abomination of desolation.
Other commentators see the abomination as lawlessness and murder
in the Temple or else as the Roman army (Luke 21:20). Whatever
the abomination was, it was a signal to flee to the mountains.

Though tragedy was coming, the good but urgent news was that
there would be time to get away for those who would not hesitate.
For those who had climbed the outside stairs and were on top of
the flat roof, there would be time to come down but not time to go
in the house to get anything (v. 15). For those in the field, there
would be time to get away but not time to pick up a coat taken off
during the heat of work (v. 16). The thought of pregnant women
and new mothers with small children trying to get away was sad
because they would not be able to move quickly (v. 17). The disciples
were to pray that the time of flight would not come in winter. Winter

was a time when rains swelled the Jordan River that had to be crossed and when those fleeing would be cold without shelter and hungry without food from the fruit trees (v. 18). If the prophecy had been about the end of the world, there would have been no need to flee or to worry about winter.

The reason for such urgent warning was that a horror point in all history was coming. The Romans later destroyed Jerusalem, the Temple, and those who did not flee in time. Since then we have experienced the holocaust of World War II when more Jews were murdered than when Jerusalem was destroyed in A.D. 70. That event has seemingly led some interpreters to focus on the exaggerative nature of the language used in word pictures of prophecy. However, there was something tragically unique about the destruction of Jerusalem. God's chosen people came under judgment in a special way (v. 19). What began as God's holy Temple was destroyed because it no longer served the holy purpose intended. (The historian Josephus has given fuller description of this destruction in his writings called the *Wars.)* So, in a sense, verse 19 can be taken very literally.

The destruction was not to be the end of God's chosen people or the end of the world. Though many would die, the destruction would come to an end; and a faithful remnant of disciples would remain. This act of mercy was prophesied as if it had already happened because it was assured that God would do what Jesus said (v. 20).

Verses 21–23 probably refer to the time indicated in verses 14–20, but they could refer to a later time. Either way, Jesus' primary concern was that his disciples not be led astray by the claims of false messiahs. Jesus had told the disciples all they needed to know before the destruction came, and he told them to watch (or take care; v. 23). The call to watchfulness appears over and over again throughout the chapter (vv. 5,9,23,33,35,37).

Signs of the Savior (13:24–27)

These verses refer to the second coming of Christ. The poetic language is drawn from Old Testament background about the Day of the Lord (see Joel 2:10; 3:15; Isa. 13:10; 34:4; Ezek. 32:7–8; Dan. 7:13; Amos 8:9). At some time after the tribulation of Jerusalem, there would come a power failure in the natural order and Jesus would come in his eternal power and glory (vv. 24–26).

When Jesus, the Son of man, comes, it will be obvious. Instead of men announcing false messiahs, the angels will gather the faithful disciples to heaven (not to the Temple).

Although verses 24–27 may draw upon numerous Old Testament passages, it may be helpful to consider these possible parallels:

(1) Verse 24 = Isaiah 13:10
(2) Verse 25 = Isaiah 34:4 (in the Greek translation)
(3) Verse 26 = Daniel 7:13–14
(4) Verse 27 = Zechariah 2:6 is implied (and a phrase from Deut. 30:4).

This conclusion still lies in the future. We have the promise of it but not a timetable or a blueprint. God is sovereign, and the choice of the end time is his—as we shall see (vv. 32–37).

A Parable of Promise (13:28–31)

The fig tree is not an evergreen; it loses its leaves in winter, and they come again in the spring. The leaves are not only a sign that summer is certain but that it is also near. Perhaps Jesus was looking at the condition of the fig trees that were on the Mount of Olives as he spoke.

The point of the comparison is stated in verses 29–30. The time factors and events are difficult to decide for sure, but we can look at the alternatives. After the fulfilling of the events of prophecy, something or someone would be near. Do the events of prophecy include verses 5–23 only? Or do they include all of verses 5–27?

The references in verses 29–30 likely refer to verses 5–23. If so, they focus on the destruction of Jerusalem and answer the question of *when* asked in verse 4 (see the commentary note on v. 4 about *all things* and *these things*). "He is near" (v. 29, RSV) may be translated "it is nigh" (KJV) and refer to the event of Jerusalem's destruction as being at hand. This view fits in with the most obvious meaning of "this generation" (v. 30), which is a reference to the people who were alive while Jesus was prophesying. Verses 5–23 only may still be intended even if the translation "he is near" (v. 29) stands. In this case, the promise would be a reassurance that in the face of destruction, Jesus is near or that his second coming could be at any time after the events of verses 5–23.

If the events of prophecy include verses 5–27, verses 29–30 would then include both the destruction of Jerusalem (vv. 5–23) and the signs of Jesus' second coming (vv. 24–27).

Verse 31 concludes the parable and its application with a ring of divine authority. The fulfillment of Jesus' prophecy is something we can depend on; it is guaranteed.

Certainties in Uncertain Times (13:32–37)

History is coming to an end, but no one knows when. The Day of the Lord, the second coming of Christ, is certain; but the time is uncertain. God the Father alone knows when this event will take place. Some theologians find it hard to accept that Jesus took some earthly limitations on himself in the matter of knowledge, but Jesus simply claimed that he did not know the time (v. 32).

Although we do not and cannot know the crucial hour, we can watch (vv. 33,35,37). Jesus used a comparison to teach the disciples that his return was certain and that they were to be good stewards while he was gone (vv. 33–36). Followers of Jesus belong to his household, and each follower has his work. The simple thought is this: When the Lord returns, you will want him to find you working, not sleeping. Each day is a gift of work and life that is to be lived in such a way that it would be fit for Jesus to see if he returned suddenly. The Romans had four watches. They were evening, midnight, cockcrow, and morning. The watches started at 6:00 P.M. and ended at 6:00 A.M. We are to live in such a way that whether the Lord comes during the night watches or during the day, we will be ready for his return.

Jesus had been speaking to the four disciples, but he added that the command to watch applied to everyone (v. 37). He gave these certainties to the four disciples and to us.

So, on the way to his death, Jesus took time to reassure his disciples of their future. His words told them all they needed to know about the future—and all we need to know. In essence, Jesus said, "Life will become black with tragedy, but do not give up. The Holy Spirit will be with you; the Father will exercise divine mercy; and I will return with great power and glory. Then we will be together for all eternity. Witness, wait, and watch" (vv. 7,9,11,13,20,23,26–27,31–37). The imagery is difficult to understand in every detail, but the central truths are clear.

Facing Death

14:1–42

Mark 14 begins what is known as the passion narrative. *Passion* basically means suffering. From this point on, Mark deals with the events that led up to the death of Christ, then his burial and resurrection. Jesus prepared himself and his disciples for his death. He was not the unwilling victim of those who plotted his death; rather, he was the obedient Son of God who fulfilled the divine plan for him to deliver mankind as the Suffering Servant Messiah (Isa. 53; Eph. 1:3–10).

We can't be dogmatic about the exact chronological order of time and events. The Romans kept time one way, and the Jews kept time another way. However, we do know the crucial steps of the story; and we can gain insights by studying parallel passages from the other Gospels (see Matt. 26; Luke 22; John 12:1 to 18:1; also see 1 Cor. 11:23–26).

Jesus both prophesied and fulfilled prophecy throughout the rest of the book of Mark. Therefore, an intermission in Mark's swift-moving drama of redemption to recall all that has gone before would be helpful before moving on to the climax. Now, after reflecting on those scenes, we come to an intense focus that sees Jesus facing death.

Plotting Murder (14:1–2)

Two days before the Passover the chief priests were wringing their hands and racking their brains for the best way to end the life of Jesus. Caiaphas, the high priest, was undoubtedly a leader in the plotting (see Matt. 26:57; John 11:47–53).

It was almost time for the Passover and the Feast of Unleavened Bread. The two feasts had merged to become one feast period that lasted a week. Passover was the most important of all Jewish feasts. Its origin lay in Israel's Exodus from Egypt (see Ex. 12:3–28; Num. 9:2–14; Deut. 16:1–8). The death angel had *passed over* the firstborn sons of the Hebrews because the blood of the lamb marked each doorpost and beam above the door as God had directed.

"Two days before the Passover" (v. 1) is hard to pinpoint, but most scholars believe it was Wednesday. Passover Day was Nisan 14 (anciently called Abib). Nisan corresponds to March or April for us. The Jewish day began at sunset or 6:00 P.M. Scholars differ in their understanding of what events took place on which days from Nisan 13–15, but the sequence of events is clear. Passover lambs were slaughtered in late afternoon, ceremonially sacrificed in the Temple, and then eaten between sunset and midnight in a family setting. It has often been noted that the sheep died for the shepherd in the Old Testament but the Shepherd died for the sheep in the New Testament (see 1 Cor. 5:7–8). Mark 14 helps us see this truth historically and in transition at the Last Supper.

Whatever the exact day was, the chief priests and scribes were plotting to murder Jesus. They never once considered the will of God in their dealings with Jesus. Long ago they had decided to destroy Jesus (Mark 3:6; 11:18; 12:12), for he had turned their compact religious world upside down. On top of that, the rulers had suffered humiliation in trying to trap Jesus verbally; so his death had become an imperative for them.

Since the Passover could be observed only in Jerusalem, pilgrims poured into the city and swelled its population by many thousands of people. Roman domination, the most important Jewish feast, and wall-to-wall people provided a tense atmosphere that could easily lead to violence. Further, Jesus was a popular person among many of those in Jerusalem (Mark 11:8–10; 12:37), and the religious leaders were about to do an unpopular thing to him. So they knew they had to arrest Jesus privately. The question was how to arrest Jesus without creating a riot. Ironically, the priests and scribes agreed they could not risk taking Jesus at the time of the feast; yet, Jesus accurately prophesied the Passover as the time for his betrayal (see Matt. 26:2). Judas' offer to betray Jesus would change their minds about the time (Mark 14:10–12).

Anointing the Anointed (14:3–9)

A lovely incident broke into the hatred that surrounded Jesus in his last days of earthly life. Jesus was eating a meal with friends at Bethany. The home was Simon the leper's; but he had undoubtedly been healed, or there wouldn't have been a banquet in his home. Mary, Martha, and Lazarus were among the guests (John 12:2–3). Suddenly Mary broke a vial of costly perfume and anointed Jesus' head and feet with it; then she wiped his feet with her hair (compare Mark 14:3 with John 12:3). Messiah means Anointed One, and Mary had anointed Jesus as the Messiah who would soon suffer death.

Judas and the other disciples at first silently resented what they counted a waste of three hundred denarii worth of perfume (see Matt. 26:8; John 12:4–5). A denarius was what a laboring man earned in one day's work. The disciples saw waste instead of a gift. They did not understand that wastefulness is hoarding something rather than using it (see Matt. 25:14–30 for the sin of doing nothing with what you have). They did not understand that love is a spendthrift that places no price tag on its choices of expression.

The silent resentment spilled over and became a noisy grumble toward Mary for wasting that which could have helped the poor (v. 5). But Jesus would not have it! He praised Mary's act as a beautiful thing and said that she had done all she could. She could not stop death, but she could lovingly anoint Jesus while he was still alive and could appreciate it. Her sense of values was personal and spiritual, not commercial. Jesus told the resentful onlookers they would always have opportunity to help the poor, but Mary had seized the unreturnable opportunity to anoint Jesus for his burial. Though her motive was loving concern, not fame, she would always be remembered for her act. All of us have limited resources and unlimited ways to spend those resources. The choice is often between what is good and what is best. Mary was sensitive and chose the unique opportunity to anoint Jesus. Arthur Hopkins once said, "There is a wealth of unexpressed love in the world. It is one of the chief causes of sorrow evoked by death: what might have been said or done that never can be said or done." Mary expressed her love while there was time. She pleased Jesus, even though her act seemed to displease everyone else. That kind of pleasing service ought to characterize every Christian's life.

Selling Out to Silver (14:10–11)

In contrast to Mary's beautiful act of anointing, Judas sold Jesus for the price of a slave (see Ex. 21:32; Matt. 26:15). Judas was the answer to the priests and scribes' puzzle (see Mark 14:1–2; John 11:57). He would know where Jesus would be when the city had gone to sleep and would point Jesus out to avoid mistaken identity at night (see John 18:2; Luke 22:6).

Why would Judas do such a thing? What got into Judas? On the surface, money was Judas' motive (see John 12:6; Matt. 26:15). Beneath the surface, there seems to have been disappointment, jealousy, ambition, and self-concern. While we do not know all the underlying motives of Judas, we do know that he chose his own will over God's will. He refused to reach the potential that Jesus had seen in him when he called him to be a disciple. And we do know that Satan got into Judas (Luke 22:3; John 13:2, 27). From that moment on, Judas joined the chief priests and scribes in their search for an opportune time to arrest Jesus.

Preparing the Passover (14:12–16)

It seems that Jesus had spent Wednesday quietly at Bethany. On Thursday the disciples asked Jesus where he wanted them to prepare the Passover meal. In response Jesus told Peter and John exactly how to find the place for supper (see Luke 22:8). He told them to follow a man carrying a pitcher of water. If a man carried water in those days, it was usually in a wineskin container. But water-carrying was considered woman's work, so a man carrying water in a pitcher would stand out like a man wearing a woman's apron in our day. The point is that the disciples would be able to easily identify the man who would lead them to Jesus' guest room (vv. 13–15). The room was Jesus' because he was to be the host and the disciples were to be his guests.

Many scholars think that Jesus had already reserved the larger upper room and that the water-carrying man was a follower of Jesus. If so, this would take nothing away from Jesus; it would simply be an example of Jesus combining his divine knowledge and human preparation for an important event. Jesus lived an orderly life that indicated advance planning and little or no hurry. It has been a popular guess that the upper room was in the home of Mary, John Mark's mother (compare Acts 12:12).

The disciples obediently found the man and the room just as Jesus had told them they would. The room was already partially prepared for the occasion. But to get completely ready for the Passover, Peter and John needed to prepare a sacrificial lamb, unleavened bread, a bowl of salt water, bitter herbs, a paste, and four cups of wine. Every detail had some symbolic meaning that reminded the Jews of their Egyptian captivity and their deliverance. Jewish writings called the Talmud give further information about Jewish observance of the Passover feast, and William Barclay has provided detailed information in his book *The Lord's Supper.*

Peter and John made preparation on Thursday afternoon. For the Jews Passover began at 6:00 P.M. (or sunset).

Exposing a Traitor (14:17–21)

When evening came, Jesus and his disciples gathered to eat the Passover. The supper began with Jesus' awful announcement that one of the twelve would betray him. One after another, the disciples painfully asked, "Surely, not I?" (Mark 14:19, author's translation). Each disciple hoped and expected that Jesus would say no, but the question came with fear and doubt.

Then Jesus dipped a morsel of food in the sauce and gave it to Judas Iscariot to expose him as the traitor (see Mark 14:20; Matt. 26:25; John 13:26–30). The prophecy of Psalm 41:9 was fulfilled. Then Judas went out (John 13:30), condemned to be the most infamous traitor of all time. He had refused to surrender to the will of God. Jesus continued to obey God's will of facing death for all mankind and offering eternal life (Mark 14:21; Isa. 53:12). Jesus' prophecy stands as a call for each reader to examine himself and avoid betraying Jesus.

Beginning a Memorial (14:22–25)

After Judas' exposure and departure, the atmosphere seemed much more relaxed. Then during the Passover observance, Jesus began the memorial we know as the Lord's Supper (see Matt. 26:26–29; Luke 22:17–20; 1 Cor. 11:23–26).

After the blessing, Jesus took the bread and said, "Take this, it means my body" (Mark 14:22, Moffatt). Then, after thanking God and giving the cup of wine to his disciples, Jesus said, "This means my covenant-blood which is shed for many" (Mark 14:24, Moffatt). Blood had symbolized the beginning of the old covenant (Ex. 24:3–8), and now blood symbolized the beginning of the new covenant (Mark 14:24). In that manner Jesus shared with his disciples the knowledge of his coming death. What he did in symbolism that Passover night, he would do in fact the next day. Jesus faced death with the certainty that the kingdom of God would come and that he would be present in the fellowship (v. 25). He had compared the kingdom of God to a banquet (Luke 14:15–24), and Mark 14:25 brings that comparison to mind. Jesus had made up his mind to drink the cup of death, and he would not drink the cup of the vine until the kingdom of God was complete.

The Lord's Supper meant that Jesus would give his body in death that mankind might have life. The Jews rightly equated blood with life; so in unmistakable words and pictures Jesus had said that he would give his life as the sacrifice for sinful man. He was the new Passover lamb for a new covenant of love, not law (Jer. 31:31–34). That was what it meant for Jesus to follow the will of God completely.

Predicting Desertion and Denial (14:26–31)

The Passover meal customarily ended with the singing of hymns of praise from the latter part of Psalms 113—118. This group of psalms is known as Hallel Psalms (or we might say Hallelujah Psalms). Then the group left for the Mount of Olives, just east of Jerusalem.

At the beginning of the supper, Jesus had announced that one of the disciples would betray him; and Judas did. At that time, each disciple had asked if he was the betrayer (Mark 14:19). But now Jesus announced that all of the disciples would desert him (a fulfillment of Zech. 13:7). This time not one disciple would admit that he might desert Jesus (Mark 14:31). Peter led the way in "knowing" that he would not desert Jesus. But Jesus prophesied that Peter would not only desert him; he would also deny him three times before a rooster would crow twice. "Cockcrow" was the name of the third Roman watch that came between midnight and 3:00 A.M. Some interpreters think of a bugle sound that announced the beginning and end of the watch, but Jesus' reference was probably to the literal crowing of a rooster.

Peter and the other disciples had trusted and followed Jesus, so it was hard for them to imagine themselves as deserters and deniers of Jesus. They could not picture themselves as sheep who would desert their shepherd (vv. 27,31).

Though the picture is pathetic, verse 28 softens the prediction by revealing that Jesus' resurrection would follow his death and that he and the disciples would be together again in Galilee. He would go before them as a shepherd would. However, the disciples never seemed to hear Jesus' prophecy of resurrection and receive that word of comfort. Notice that Jesus was to be *raised* (v. 28). The same power that raised Jesus will raise his followers—namely, the power of God (see Acts 2:23–24).

Willing God's Will (14:32–42)

Gethsemane lay at the foot of the Mount of Olives. It was the scene of agony and victory. There Jesus faced again the alternative of avoiding death. He had been tempted time and again to set up a messiahship that did not involve the cross and to provide salvation without atonement. In fact, his ministry began with that temptation (Mark 1:12–13). But each time, he resisted the alternative and gave himself completely to carrying out the full plan of his Father.

At this cruel hour Jesus withdrew from man to be with God. He left eight of the disciples at the edge of Gethsemane. He took Peter, James, and John—the Mount of Transfiguration disciples—deeper into Gethsemane with him. They had had a glimpse of Jesus' glory (Mark 9:2–8); now they were to have a glimpse of the unique suffering that Jesus would undergo before further glory would come (Mark 14:33–34). Peter had vowed he would not desert or deny Jesus (see Mark 14:29,66–72). James and John had said that they were able to drink Jesus' cup (Mark 10:35–39). But Jesus knew what they were about to face in the way of temptation to desert him and to abandon their discipleship. So he wanted them to watch and pray (vv. 34,37–38, 41). But each time Jesus returned from praying, he found them asleep.

After sharing how troubled he was and asking Peter, James, and John to watch, Jesus moved further into Gethsemane. However, he did not move beyond their hearing, and it was customary to pray aloud. So between their times of sleeping, the disciples would have heard Jesus' prayer.

Jesus intimately prayed to God with the warm and affectionate Aramaic term *Abba* for Father (v. 36). This is the first record of the term Abba being used in prayer to God. It expressed the unique relationship between God the Father and God the Son. Jesus prayed for the hour to pass and the cup to be delivered from him (vv. 35–36). The two requests were for the same thing. The persistent prayer of Jesus was for God to remove the need for him to bear the sin of the world in undeserved death. His life was untainted by the sin that separated mankind from God. Jesus looked into the hour and the cup, and he saw the horror of sin that he was to bear. That awful weight was crushing him. But Jesus' decision proved that he wanted one thing more than he wanted to escape sin's guilt and death: He wanted the will of his Father to be done (v. 36). The will of God was for the sinless Jesus to die on the cross for the sins of all mankind.

When Jesus' agony was over, his peace was complete. He emerged with calmness and majesty, ready to face trial, physical death, and redemption for man's sin. His faith remained victorious. He found the disciples sleeping a third time and told them that everything was settled (v. 41). He had prayed the temptation through; Judas the betrayer was approaching; and Jesus was ready to face death head-on. He did not run from it, for he knew that it was the will of God.

The pattern of Jesus' life is the pattern for all of us. In every area of life, the Christian is to submit his will to the will of God—regardless of what the consequences might be.

Giving Up Life
14:43 to 15:41

To supplement Mark's brief, quick-moving account, it is especially important to study the other Gospels for details and helpful insights. Mark 14:43 to 15:41 is paralleled as follows: (1) Matthew 26:47 to 27:56; (2) Luke 22:47 to 23:49; (3) John 18:2 to 19:30. These passages move from the betrayal of Jesus, through the trials and crucifixion, to Jesus' victorious death.

When Jesus finished his praying, he was completely ready for all that lay before him. He knew that what God willed for him was good news for mankind. What he would accomplish would give believers reason for joy and would challenge nonbelievers to turn their lives over to God. As Jesus rejoined his disciples, Judas was coming into Gethsemane.

A Cowardly Arrest (14:43–52)

The city slept and the moon was full when Judas led the Sanhedrin guard to seize Jesus. The Sanhedrin was made up of the high priest, former high priests (chief priests), and others who were called elders and scribes. This Jewish supreme court had access to a Temple police force that could act within certain limitations under Roman law. For example, they could arrest, but they could not execute anyone. Judas, the Temple police, members of the Sanhedrin (see Luke 22:52–53), and perhaps others came together. There is divided opinion over whether the band included Roman soldiers (but see John 18:3). Regardless of the question about Roman soldiers, the focus was on the Jewish element.

Judas led the way as the crowd came to hunt Jesus with swords, clubs, lanterns, and torches (Mark 14:43; Luke 22:47; John 18:3). Though the moon was full at the Passover season, the rugged terrain would provide shadows and caves for a fugitive to hide in; but Jesus voluntarily met the mob. And Judas played his infamous role by calling Jesus "Master!" and by giving him a fervent kiss. It was customary for pupils to greet their teachers with a kiss, but Judas' kiss was an act of hypocrisy that served as an agreed-upon sign to identify Jesus to those who would arrest him (v. 44).

At the signal of the kiss, the police seized Jesus. Peter, who seemingly never stifled an impulse, drew his sword and sliced off Malchus' right ear instead of his head, which Peter undoubtedly had intended to cut off (see John 18:10). Only Luke the physician reveals that Jesus healed the ear of Malchus, servant of the high priest (see Luke 22:50–51). God willed for Jesus to give his life, not for it to be taken from him. So Jesus told Peter to put up his sword (John 18:11). But Jesus was righteously indignant that his arresters would come after him as after a common criminal (v. 48). He was not a robber or a person guilty of rebellion; he was the Son of God who had taught daily in the Temple and could have been arrested there (v. 49).

But Jesus recognized that prophecy was being fulfilled (see Ps. 41:9; Isa. 53:12). Then all the disciples deserted Jesus (v. 50) as he had prophesied in Mark 14:27 (see also Zech. 13:7). While Jesus remained calm, the disciples panicked and ran. All left Jesus for whom they had once left all. Verses 51–52 tell of a young disciple who may have been the last to run away and who nearly got caught. The young man was probably John Mark himself. If the Last Supper was in the home of Mary, his mother, he may have dressed hurriedly and followed Jesus and his disciples. That would account for the scant clothing that was grasped as he ran away naked. If this was the case, it was Mark's humble way of saying, "I was there, and I also deserted him."

A Judicial Farce (14:53–65)

Jesus had two trials with three stages each according to the collective record of the Gospels: a religious trial and a civil trial. These verses focus on the religious trial. Jesus was first brought to Annas, who was a former high priest and was father-in-law to Caiaphas (John 18:12–14,19–24). Caiaphas was the current high priest and president of the Sanhedrin, which was the Jewish supreme court. After Annas, high priest emeritus, questioned Jesus, the Sanhedrin led by Caiaphas tried Jesus once informally and then again formally. The charge became blasphemy, but the whole process was a judicial farce.

A kangaroo court (vv. 53–54).—The Sanhedrin broke its own rules. It could not meet legally until sunrise; nor could the court meet at any of the great feasts. They broke these rules and others. Anyone can see that the court's interest was injustice, not justice. They had prejudged Jesus long before the court ever met (see Mark 14:1).

A verse about Peter breaks in so abruptly that it seems out of place (v. 54). However, the verse merely shows what was happening to Peter while Jesus was being tried. John seems to have been with Peter (see John 18:15–16). After this brief interlude, Jesus' trial resumed.

Lying witnesses (vv. 55–59).—The court had trouble getting a charge that would condemn Jesus to death. At least two witnesses had to agree on a specific charge to make an accusation stick (Num. 35:30; Deut. 17:6; 19:15). The trouble didn't come from lack of evidence but from too much evidence. (In fact, the number of witnesses in the middle of the night indicates something of the plotting that had been involved in arresting and trying Jesus.) The false witnesses could not agree on a consistent lie. When two of the false witnesses tried to tell the truth, they couldn't even get the truth straight. (Contrast the exact wording of Mark 14:58 with Matt. 26:61 and John 2:19.) The witnesses had to testify individually and could not differ in details, and no two passed that test.

A blinding truth (vv. 60–65).—Jesus' silence and refusal to defend himself against the false witnesses annoyed Caiaphas (v. 60). Since none of the charges so far merited a death sentence and since the witnesses had disqualified themselves, Caiaphas insisted that Jesus answer under oath whether he was the Messiah, the Son of God (Mark 14:61; Matt. 26:63). At that point Jesus condemned himself with the truth: "I am" (v. 62). The statement was probably just an answer of yes, but the answer was also the title of God himself (Ex. 3:14). Jesus made it easy for his accusers when he further described the evidence that proved he was the Messiah (see Mark 14:62). This announcement would have been familiar (see Ps. 110:1; Dan. 7:13–14). Scholars differ over whether verse 62 refers to Jesus' ascension or his second coming; the latter seems to fit the language of Mark.

Without even considering Jesus' claim, the biased Sanhedrin agreed that there was no need for further witnesses. The high priest ripped his clothes in the way prescribed when blasphemy had occurred. Blasphemy was punishable by death (Lev. 24:16), and the Sanhedrin formally pronounced that death sentence—though it did not have the power to carry out the death sentence (see John 18:31). However, it would be easy for the religious leaders to change Jesus' admission of messiahship to King of the Jews and bring the political charge of treason against him before civil authorities.

The people began to spit on him contemptuously and beat him. They covered his face and asked him to prophesy who it was that had hit him (see Matt. 26:68; Luke 22:63–64). Even the guards hit him as they took him. It was a sick scene.

A Denying Disciple (14:66–72)

By the warmth and light of the courtyard fire, a maidservant of the high priest questioned Peter and then accused him of being Jesus' disciple (Mark 14:66–67; John 18:17–18). He gave an awkward double denial and moved away. Soon the maid saw Peter again and insisted he was one of Jesus' disciples. Peter repeatedly denied the charge. The unmistakable Galilean speech gave him away. Galileans had trouble with guttural sounds and pronounced sounds such as *sh* with *th*. Other bystanders took up the maid's accusations. One of them was a relative of Malchus, and Peter had cut off Malchus' ear (Mark 14:47; John 18:25–26). When the accusations became more than Peter could bear, he called a curse upon himself if he were not telling the truth; and he promptly denied Jesus a third time. At that instant Peter heard the second cock crow (trumpet or rooster sound) and found himself face to face with Jesus (Luke 22:60–62). As Peter's mind flashed back over the night's events, his heart was broken. He sobbed loudly and cried bitter tears over his sin.

The vivid details have the ring of personal testimony, which Peter must have shared with John Mark. The one Jesus had nicknamed Rock (Peter) was more like jelly at that time. However, he would later live up to the name Jesus gave him.

The scene ended with the prophecy of Mark 14:29–31 having been fulfilled. Morning was coming quickly, and the religious court would be exchanged for a civil court.

Changing Courts and Charges (15:1-5)

At first light the Sanhedrin legalized its informal night meeting by rubber-stamping the earlier condemnation of Jesus. Then because of Roman domination that decreed Jews could not carry out the death sentence, the Jewish leaders decided to take Jesus from their religious court to Pilate's civil court—probably about 6:00 A.M. (See the parallels in Matt. 27:2,11-14; Luke 23:1-5; John 18:28-38.) The civil trial had three stages: Jesus was brought to Pilate, sent to Herod (Luke 23:6-12), and returned to Pilate. It was sad irony that the Jewish religious leaders failed to recognize and accept their Messiah; instead, they accused him of blasphemy and then led the Messiah the Jews had looked for to the Gentiles to get him put to death. Later, the chief priests were to say, "We have no king but Caesar" (John 19:15).

In the eyes of Rome the charge of blasphemy, which the Jews had pronounced, would not merit a death sentence from the civil court. So the Sanhedrin played down blasphemy and charged Jesus with treason. The charges would have been formally stated in writing or orally. While Jesus agreed to accept the title "King of the Jews," which Pilate stated, he did not agree to the charge of treason (see Mark 15:2; John 18:33-37).

Actually, the accusing leaders made four specific charges against Jesus: (1) stirring up people against Rome, (2) prohibiting the poll tax, (3) claiming to be a king, and (4) claiming to be the Son of God (Luke 23:2; John 19:7). The first two charges were lies, and the last two charges were unrecognized truths about Jesus.

Mark 15:2 reveals that the Jewish leaders had twisted Jesus' admission of being the Messiah into a political charge: They accused him of claiming to be a king. If Jesus had set himself up as a rival against Caesar, that would have been considered high treason. However, Pilate was not dumb. Except for a brief reply to Pilate, Jesus had remained silent as the Suffering Servant (Mark 15:2-5; Isa. 53:7). Pilate hated the Jews, and they hated him; and Pilate knew the charges against Jesus smelled fishy (Mark 15:5,10). After questioning Jesus, Pilate could tell that Jesus was not guilty of treason or of anything else (see John 18:33-38).

When Pilate heard that Jesus was a Galilean, he sent him to Herod Antipas, the Galilean ruler (Luke 23:5-12). It was not unusual to send an accused person before his home court for trial. And, as it happened, Herod was in Jerusalem. But instead of judging Jesus, Herod ridiculed him and returned him to Pilate without any condemnation. As a matter of fact, neither Pilate nor Herod could see that Jesus was guilty of any wrong. But their acquittal of Jesus did not result in Jesus' release.

A Condemning Crowd (15:6–15)

Pilate tried to have a good conscience and appease the crowd too. The other Gospels enlarge on this picture of how Pilate wavered (Matt. 27:15–26; Luke 23:13–25; John 18:39 to 19:16). Now the people were crying for their annual gift: at Passover the Roman governor released any *one* prisoner the people wanted released (v. 8). Pilate took this custom as a possible way out of the problem of what to do with Jesus. He knew Jesus' enemies wanted him dead because they envied his influence and popularity (v. 10), but he hoped the people would want the popular Jesus released (see Mark 12:37). However, when Pilate offered Jesus, the crowd chose Barabbas. The chief priests had stirred up the crowd against Jesus (v. 11). So there was no chanting for Jesus. Further, the crowds threatened Pilate's position by indicating that a choice for Jesus would be considered a choice against Caesar (John 19:10). And the Jews had influence in Rome.

That decided the matter for the weak and cowardly Pilate (John 19:13–16). He listened to the cry of the crowds; at the same time, he turned a deaf ear to the truth and to his wife's advice (Matt. 27:19). It would do no good for Pilate to wash his hands (Matt. 27:24); he too was guilty of Jesus' death.

Jesus was judged guilty by the religious leaders for the very thing he refused to be: a political messiah. Though innocent of treason, Jesus took the place of Barabbas, a known murderer, thief, and insurrectionist (Mark 15:7; John 19:40). Barabbas was guilty of what Jesus was accused of, and he was probably popular with the Zealots. But Pilate knowingly freed a guilty man and condemned an innocent one (Mark 15:15). Then Pilate immediately had Jesus whipped as the customary first step toward crucifixion (see Isa. 53:6,12). There was no set limit on the number of strokes for the whipping. The scourging was done with a leather whip lined with metal or bone, so it was brutal and could even result in death. After the whipping, Pilate handed Jesus over to the soldiers and to the crowd for crucifixion. Pilate's act was a formal death sentence for Jesus.

Crucifixion meant a cruel death on a cross. The death involved the pain of a body torn by nails, exposure to the weather, and—if it lasted long enough—hunger and thirst. The Jews executed by stoning a person to death (see Deut. 13:10; Acts 7:58). The Romans usually beheaded their citizens who were executed. They saved crucifixion for slaves and foreigners and for the crime of high treason. Since Jesus was accused of setting himself up as a rival to Emperor Tiberius Caesar, the charge was high treason. High treason could be punished by crucifixion, death by wild beasts in an arena, or by exile. The crowds had cried for crucifixion, and Pilate agreed to give the crowds what they wanted.

A Redeeming Death (15:16–41)

A predeath mockery (vv. 16–20).—While the cross was being prepared, the soldiers treated the real King with mock royalty. They stripped Jesus and costumed him as a king: a purple cloak as a sign of royalty, a woven circle of thorns for a crown, and a reed in his right hand for a scepter. Then they mockingly saluted Jesus as a king of the Jews and knelt before him. They spit on him, and they took the reed and hit him on the head with it. After that ridicule, they put Jesus' own clothes on him and led him away to be crucified.

Crucifixion (vv. 21–28).—Golgotha was the site of the crucifixion. It is the Aramaic word for *place of a skull.* Calvary is the Latin translation of Golgotha, and it means *a bare skull.* Jesus began the trip to Golgotha by carrying his own crosspiece (John 19:17). Since he had already been unmercifully beaten, he must have fallen exhausted beneath the cross's heavy load. So the soldiers forced Simon of Cyrene to take up Jesus' cross and carry it. Simon was identified as the father of Alexander and Rufus. The father and two sons must have been well known to Mark and his readers (see Rom. 16:13). Cyrene was in North Africa; it was a Greek settlement that had many Jews. Cyrenians are also mentioned in Acts 6:9; 11:20; 13:1. Was Simon a pilgrim who had come to Jerusalem for the Passover feast? Or was he a resident of Jerusalem? Was he black? Why was he chosen? No one knows the answer to these questions for sure. We do know that this passerby literally took up the cross of Jesus; and there is the implication that he and his sons became disciples of Jesus who continued to bear the cross symbolically (compare Mark 8:34).

Jesus was offered wine drugged with myrrh that would have eased his pain, but he refused it and took the full force of the pain of crucifixion (see Prov. 31:6–7; Mark 14:25). Finally they crucified Jesus! Proph-

ecy was fulfilled, and Jesus provided salvation for all who would commit their lives to him. The shame of the cross became good news
for sinful mankind (see Rom. 1:16).

Beneath the cross, soldiers divided the garments they were supposed to get from the one they crucified. However, when they came
to Jesus' seamless tunic, they threw dice for it (see John 19:23–24;
Ps. 22:18). Exact time factors are hard to pinpoint; but according to
Mark the crucifixion began about 9:00 A.M. (the third hour by Jewish
time).

Attached to the cross was the written reason given for Jesus' crucifixion: "The King of the Jews." The charge was written in Hebrew,
Greek, and Latin so that everyone could read what it said. Pilate
would not alter the inscription to suit the chief priests (see John 19:19–
22).

Along with Jesus, two other men were crucified. They occupied
the places that James and John had naively asked for (Mark 10:35–
38). The two men were identified as robbers (v. 27), and it is likely
that they were also guilty of treason since they were being put to
death. It is possible that they were accomplices of Barabbas. (Verse
28 is not in the best texts and is omitted from the RSV.)

Suffering and death (vv. 29–41).—The crowds laughed at Jesus'
seeming helplessness, and they recalled the earlier distorted charge
that Jesus would destroy the Temple and raise it in three days (see
Mark 14:58; 15:29–30; and the exact words of Jesus in John 2:19–
21). Then the religious leaders sadistically said that Jesus saved others
but could not save himself. Jesus had saved others from every kind
of trouble, but what the chief priests said was true—in a way they
would not understand: Jesus could save others only by staying on
the cross and not saving himself. The chief priests sarcastically urged
Jesus to come down so that they could see and believe. In the spiritual
realm the order is first to believe and then to see. But the religious
leaders were not interested in believing; they were interested in Jesus'
death, which they had wanted for a long time (see Mark 3:6; 11:18;
12:12; 14:1,64). Along with the crowds and religious leaders, even
Jesus' fellow-sufferers taunted him—though one of the two would later
find salvation (see Luke 23:39–43).

Unexplainable darkness came at noon and lasted until 3:00 P.M.
We can never know how dark it was for Jesus in those hours, but
we do know that the unclouded communion between Father and
Son was broken during that time. None of Jesus' physical pain com-

pared with his pain of bearing the world's sin. The "Calvary Psalm" (Ps. 22) begins with agony and ends with victory; and Jesus quoted those first words: "My God, my God, why hast thou forsaken me?" (Ps. 22:1). We can only know that the cost of our salvation was indescribable suffering that called for the sinless Jesus to take our sin upon himself. God's grace has never been cheap or simple, but it has come to us as the gift of salvation through Jesus Christ (Eph. 2:8–10).

When Jesus had cried out the words of Psalm 22:1, he spoke them with the Aramaic, "Eloi, Eloi, lama sabachthani?" (Mark 15:34). And some of the bystanders thought he was calling on Elijah to deliver him from the cross (v. 35). Someone offered Jesus a vinegar drink when he cried out in thirst and perhaps because they wanted to help him stay conscious (Mark 15:36; John 19:28–30). Then, while the misunderstanding bystanders waited to see if Elijah would come, Jesus said victoriously: "It is finished" (John 19:30). "Father, into thy hands I commit my spirit!" (Luke 23:46). And somehow Jesus seemed to give up his life voluntarily as he released his last breath.

At the moment Jesus died, the earth shook and the curtain of the Temple split from top to bottom (Mark 15:38; Matt. 27:51). There were two curtains or veils in the Temple: one at the entrance to the Temple itself and one that hung between the holy place and the holy of holies. If the curtain that split was the one that led to the holy of holies, it was symbolic of Jesus' gift of direct access to God. For up until that time only the high priest was to go into the holy of holies, and that was only on the Day of Atonement (see Lev. 16). Jesus provided direct access to God for every worshiper. If the curtain that split was the one at the entrance to the Temple, it could signify an end to Judaism and a warning that the destruction of the Temple was forthcoming. Either way, Jesus' death and the splitting of the curtain announced that things would never be the same again. There was a new day of faith and a new covenant.

The majestic way Jesus died led the Roman centurion to say, "Truly this man was the Son of God" (Mark 15:39, KJV). And faithful women disciples watched.

From beginning to end, we have seen man's weakness and Jesus' strength, man's sin and Jesus' sinlessness, man's unjustness and Jesus' justness. Because every person has sinned, every person has in some way shared in the crucifixion of Christ. Yet, in spite of our sinful nature, Jesus loved us and willingly gave his life for us.

Salvation Symphony
15:42 to 16:20

Although the literal darkness of the hours Jesus spent on the cross
had lifted with his death, gloom still darkened the hearts of Jesus'
followers; for their Messiah was dead, and their hope was gone. Usually, with the death of a book's central figure, nothing would be left
but anticlimax. However, what is left in the book of Mark builds from
a humanitarian request and deep despair to an incredible, climactic
announcement of good news. Mark 16:6 causes us to remember Mark
1:1 and all that has happened in between.

Musical compositions often move from the dark, mournful notes
of a minor key to a mighty crescendo of triumphant, harmonious
sounds. The salvation symphony is like that as it moves from burial
and mourning to the golden daybreak of Jesus' resurrection.

Burying the Messiah (15:42–46)

Critical timing (v. 42).—Jesus died about 3:00 P.M. on Friday afternoon, the day of preparation for the sabbath. Since the Jewish sabbath
began at 6:00 P.M. on Friday evening, Jesus' burial presented a time
problem for anyone who would want to give him a proper burial.
Further, touching a dead body made a Jew ceremonially unclean
for seven days; so to bury Jesus on the sabbath would put those friends
of Jesus in a position of being unable to take part in the sabbath or
the religious festivities which would begin in a few hours. Although
the Romans had crucified Jesus, it was the Jews who had demanded
the crucifixion. The Romans did not care how long a body hung on
a cross. However, by Moses' law an executed criminal was not supposed to remain on a tree (or cross) overnight (see Deut. 21:22–23).
That fact explains why the Jewish leaders wanted to speed up the
death of Jesus and the other two on the crosses (also see John 19:31).

Belated bravery (v. 43).—Joseph of Arimathea asked Pilate for the
privilege of burying Jesus' body. Technically, Jesus' body belonged
to the Roman government, as did the bodies of all executed criminals.
The Romans usually left a body to decay on the cross unless friends
or relatives asked for burial permission.

Joseph was a wealthy, respected member of the Sanhedrin; however, he had not agreed to the death of Jesus (see Luke 23:50–51). No doubt, Joseph's grief was great because he had been a secret disciple and had failed to follow the living Jesus; now he was left with only a memory.

Though Joseph's bravery was belated, he now openly and courageously took his public stand for Jesus (Matt. 27:57; Luke 23:52–54; John 19:38). Joseph's Jewish colleagues had threatened to expel from the synagogue anyone who followed Jesus. Nevertheless, the death that had wrecked the brave resolutions of the disciples gave timid Joseph the boldness to identify himself to the Romans as a disciple of Jesus who wanted the privilege of burying his body. Joseph had waited for the reign of God (the kingdom of God). Now his actions showed that the kingdom of God had come into his own life. Though the kingdom of God has a future sense to it, it also has a present sense to those whose lives boldly and openly show that Jesus Christ is the Lord of their lives.

Prompt death (vv. 44–45).—When Joseph came asking for Jesus' body only six hours after the crucifixion, Pilate was amazed. He wondered if it was possible that Jesus could already be dead. Crucified criminals almost never died in less than two to three days, and some lingered as long as three to six days. Death often came from exposure and exhaustion rather than from the wounds of crucifixion. Pilate sent for the centurion who had presided over the crucifixion to get an official report about whether Jesus was dead or alive. The centurion didn't have any doubt about the matter; he knew. And he assured Pilate that Jesus was dead. And, after all, who should be more certain than the Roman centurion in charge of the crucifixion? As a matter of record, everyone at the cross knew that Jesus was dead; and no one expected him to live again on this earth. When Pilate was convinced that Jesus was dead, he freely and gladly granted Joseph the body of Jesus for burial.

Pilate's personal decisions about Jesus were based on what others wanted him to do with Jesus. So Pilate gave away Jesus' life in the morning and his body in the afternoon. But Pilate never claimed Jesus for his own Lord and Savior. And many people today make the same mistakes Pilate made by letting others negatively influence their decisions about what to do with Jesus.

A hurried burial (v. 46).—The time was probably about 4:00 P.M., and only two hours remained for the burial before the Jewish sabbath, which began at 6:00 P.M. In that short time Joseph hurried to remove Jesus' body from the cross and to give him a royal burial. Joseph had the help of Nicodemus (another secret disciple turned bold by the cross of Jesus). Others may have helped also. The preparation for the burial shows that Joseph and Nicodemus had worked together (see John 19:38–42). Joseph brought the fine linen material to wrap the body, and Nicodemus brought about one hundred pounds of spices to crumble between the strips of linen cloth. Next, Joseph and Nicodemus reverently placed Jesus' body in Joseph's nearby tomb.

The tomb was new, unused, and cut out of the rock. It was the kind of tomb that a wealthy family would have. They laid Jesus there. Then they rolled the huge, grindstonelike rock downhill into its place at the entrance of the tomb. The stone was in a groove and provided an effective seal against men or animals who might want to disturb Jesus' body (see also Matt. 27:62–66). Jesus would not be in the tomb long, but Joseph and Nicodemus did not know that. They spent a large amount of money with the thought that they were burying Jesus in a tomb forever—not just for three days. That was Friday; the sabbath was about to begin (it lasted Friday evening and until 6:00 P.M. on Saturday).

Mourning the Messiah (15:47 to 16:4)

Burdened planning (15:47).—Faithful women had watched their dreams and hopes die when Jesus died (see Mark 15:40). They had followed Jesus from the trial to Golgotha to the tomb. The women, with their deep love for Jesus, were still there when everyone else had gone. Mark mentioned that Mary Magdalene and Mary, the mother of Jesus, watched to see where Jesus was buried. They watched with a purpose, for they planned to pay their final respects to Jesus' body by anointing it at a later time.

Loving care (16:1–2).—The women rested on the sabbath, according to the commandment (Luke 23:56). But when the sabbath ended, they bought spices to anoint Jesus' body. Then their devotion to the crucified Master—whom they knew to be dead—led them to the tomb at the earliest possible moment on Sunday (the third day since Jesus' burial by Jewish reckoning). The women had to travel about two miles, so they set out in darkness and arrived just at sunrise (see also John 20:1; Luke 24:1).

Unneeded concern (16:3–4).—The mourners were concerned all the way to the grave because they knew they could not budge the huge stone. Putting the stone in place was relatively easy because it fit in a groove and was rolled downhill, but removing the stone would require rolling it uphill. So they approached the sepulcher with downcast spirits and downcast eyes. But when they looked up, they saw the stone completely removed from the doorway of the grave. The stone was so big that they could see it from a distance. (Matthew tells us that an angel had rolled the stone away—Matt. 28:2–4.)

A Resurrected Messiah (16:5–8)

A surprise (v. 5).—When the women got into the tomb, Jesus' body was gone and an angel was sitting on the right side of the tomb (see Matt. 28:5). The women were alarmed and distressed. They thought Jesus' body had been stolen.

An announcement (v. 6).—In essence the angel said, "Calm down! I know you are looking for the crucified body of Jesus of Nazareth; but he is not here because *he is risen!*" Then the angel told the women to look at the place where Joseph and Nicodemus had laid Jesus. Empty! The burial clothes were there (John 20:5–7), but Jesus was not there. They no longer had only a loving memory of a dead Jesus; now they had the living presence of the resurrected Messiah. The angel's announcement was a revelation that meant Jesus is alive forevermore. He had risen as he said he would (Mark 8:31; 9:31; 10:34; 14:28). The point of faith is the resurrection, not just the empty tomb.

When Christ conquered death, he gave all mankind the possibility of life beyond the grave. His defeat of death guarantees eternal life, which begins now, for all who believe in Christ as Lord and Savior. The quality of life begins with commitment to Christ and continues through time and death and eternity.

A task (vv. 7–8).—The angel commanded the women to tell the disciples and Peter about the resurrection and about Jesus' plan to meet the disciples in Galilee (see Mark 14:28). Peter was still a disciple, but he needed special mention to reassure him of that fact and to help him overcome the deep humiliation involved in his denial of Jesus. The women were seized with emotion: fear, trembling, astonishment, and joy (Matt. 28:8).

In the best, oldest manuscripts, the Gospel of Mark ends at verse 8 with the fearful women fleeing the tomb in dumbfounded silence.

The other Gospels reveal that the women carried out the command of the angel to tell the others the good news (Matt. 28:8; Luke 24:8–12; John 20:2). All Christians share the task assigned to the women of telling others the good news about eternal life through the risen Christ.

Epilogue (16:9–20)

Afraid (v. 8) does not appear to be a good word to end an account of good news. And though the oldest and best manuscripts do end with Mark 16:8, verses 9–20 and another ending began to show up very early in other manuscripts. Scholars differ on whether Mark intended to stop at 16:8, but they largely agree that what we have in 16:9–20 was not written by Mark. Five viewpoints summarize most thinking about the ending of the Gospel of Mark:

1. Mark completed his Gospel with 16:8 even though the ending is abrupt.
2. The original ending of the Gospel of Mark may have been torn off at the end of the scroll.
3. Mark could have been interrupted and not gotten to finish all that he wanted to write in the inspired record.
4. Verses 9–20 are considered by some to be a part of the original Gospel of Mark.
5. Verse 8 could have had a different ending as indicated in *The New English Bible:* "And they delivered all these instructions briefly to Peter and his companions. Afterwards Jesus himself sent out by them from east to west the sacred and imperishable message of eternal salvation."

This writer believes that the first or second alternatives are the most probable choices. But because we are almost two thousand years removed from the original writing, no one knows exactly how Mark ended his book. We do know that Jesus' tomb was empty and that Jesus appeared to his disciples on a number of occasions after his resurrection. Paul most concisely told about resurrection appearances and the meaning of the whole Christ event (in 1 Cor. 15:3–8).

It seems important to take a summary look at Mark 16:9–20 regardless of whether the verses originally appeared in Mark's Gospel. Most of the content in those verses appears elsewhere in the Gospels or in Acts. The breakdown of verses 9–20 and their possible counterparts elsewhere may be helpful:

Verses 9–11: Appearance to Mary Magdalene (see Luke 24:10–11, 22–24; John 20:11–18; and possibly John 20:1–2).

Verses 12–13: Appearance to the two travelers (see Luke 24:13–35).

Verses 14–18: Appearance to the eleven (see Luke 24:36–49; Matt. 28:16–20; and parts of the book of Acts).

Verses 19–20: Ascension and continued activity (see Acts 1:9–11).

Scholars see other parallels in addition to the ones just listed, but the heart of Mark 16:9–20 is reflected in the passages cited. Readers will share different concerns about the verses that likely were not in Mark's original Gospel and which may not have support elsewhere in the New Testament: for example, drinking something deadly or picking up serpents (v. 18). And it does not seem wise to build a theological position on these verses alone. But, speaking positively, verses 9–20 call Christians to preach and minister in the power of the resurrected Christ, who did not leave his disciples alone to continue his work.

As for Mark's Gospel, we have now come to the end of Mark's record about Jesus. But the end of that story is only a beginning for those who turn from their sin and put their whole trust in Jesus as Lord and Savior. Mark's Gospel is not a biography. It is good news that calls for every person to decide what he will personally do with Jesus Christ. The essential truth is this: Jesus Christ is God's good news for mankind, and Jesus alone is the way to eternal life. Outside of Christ there is only spiritual death. So life's crucial question is this: What will you do with Jesus?

Bibliography

General Works

Barclay, William. *The First Three Gospels.* London: SCM Press LTD, 1966.
Barclay, William. *The Lord's Supper.* Nashville: Abingdon Press, 1967.
Hester, H. I. *The Heart of the New Testament.* Liberty, Missouri: William Jewel Press, 1950.
Stewart, James S. *The Life and Teaching of Jesus Christ.* New York: Abingdon Press.

Commentaries

Allen, Clifton J., gen. ed. *The Broadman Bible Commentary* 8. Nashville: Broadman Press, 1969.
Barclay, William. *And Jesus Said: A Handbook on the Parables of Jesus.* 121 George Street, Edinburgh: The Church of Scotland Youth Committee, 1960.
Barclay, William. *The Daily Study Bible* 3: *The Gospel of Mark.* Philadelphia: Westminster Press, 1956.
Barnes, Albert. *Notes on the New Testament: Matthew and Mark.* Grand Rapids: Baker Book House, 1958.
Bruce, A. B. *The Expositor's Greek Testament* 1. Grand Rapids: William B. Eerdmans Publishing Co., 1951.
Clark, William N., *An American Commentary on the New Testament* 2: *Mark and Luke.* Philadelphia: American Baptist Publication Society, 1881.
Cole, Allan. *Tyndale Bible Commentaries* 2: *The Gospel According to St. Mark.* Grand Rapids: William B. Eerdmans Publishing Co., 1961.
Elliott, Melvin E. *The Language of the King James Bible.* Garden City, New York: Doubleday & Co., Inc., 1967.
Erdman, Charles R. *The Gospel of Mark.* Philadelphia: Westminster Press, 1964.
Findlay, J. Alexander. *Jesus and His Parables.* London: The Epworth Press, 1957.
Gould, Ezra P. *The International Critical Commentary: The Gospel According to St. Mark.* Edinburgh: T & T Clark, 1896.

Hamilton, William. *The Modern Reader's Guide to Mark*. New York: Association Press, 1959.

Hunter, A. M. *The Gospel According to Saint Mark*. New York: Collier Books, 1962.

Jeremias, Joachim. *Rediscovering the Parables*. New York: Charles Scribner's Sons, 1966. Copyright held by SCM Press LTD, London.

Lane, William L. *The New International Commentary on the New Testament: Commentary on the Gospel of Mark*. Grand Rapids: William B. Eerdmans Publishing Co., 1974.

Leitch, James W. *The King Comes: An Exposition of Mark 1—7*. London: SCM Press LTD, 1965.

Lockyer, Herbert. *All the Books and Chapters of the Bible*. Grand Rapids: Zondervan Publishing House, 1966.

Maclear, G. F., ed. *Cambridge Greek Testament for Schools and Colleges*. Cambridge: University of Cambridge Press, 1909.

Minear, Paul S. *The Layman's Bible Commentary* 17. Richmond: John Knox Press, 1962.

Moule, C. F. D. *The Cambridge Bible Commentary on the New English Bible: The Gospel According to St. Mark*. Cambridge: Cambridge University Press, 1965.

Robertson, A. T. *A Harmony of the Gospels*. Nashville: Broadman Press, 1922.

Robertson, A. T. *Word Pictures in the New Testament* 1. Nashville: Broadman Press, 1930.

Stalker, James. *The Life of Jesus Christ*. Westwood, New Jersey: Fleming H. Revell Co., 1949.

Swete, Henry Barclay. *The Gospel According to St. Mark*. Grand Rapids: William B. Eerdmans Publishing Co., 1956.

Taylor, Vincent. *The Gospel According to St. Mark*. London: Macmillan & Co. LTD, 1959; New York: St. Martin's Press, 1959.

Wuest, Kenneth S. *Mark in the Greek New Testament*. Grand Rapids: William B. Eerdmans Publishing Co., 1955.

Dictionaries, Encyclopedias, and Lexicons

Arndt, William F., and Gingrich, F. Wilbur. *A Greek-English Lexicon of the New Testament*. Chicago: The University of Chicago Press, 1957.

Souter, Alexander. *A Pocket Lexicon to the Greek New Testament*. London: Oxford University Press, 1916.

Thayer, Joseph Henry. *A Greek-English Lexicon of the New Testament*. New York: American Book Company, 1886. Copyright held by Harper and Brothers, New York, 1889.

The International Standard Bible Encyclopedia. Grand Rapids: William B. Eerdmans Publishing Co., 1939.

The Interpreter's Dictionary of the Bible. New York: Abingdon Press, 1962.

Von Allmen, J. J., ed. *A Companion to the Bible.* New York: Oxford University Press, 1958.

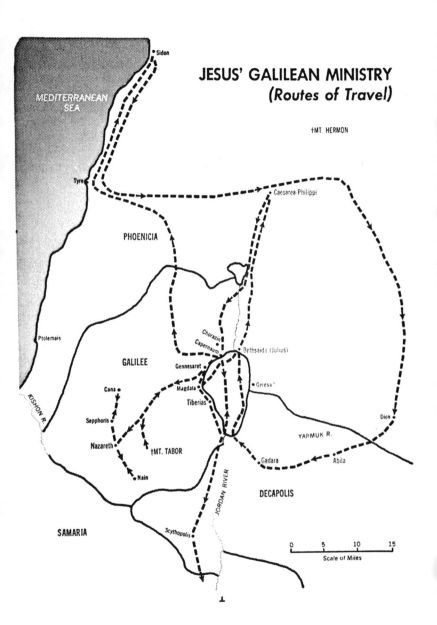

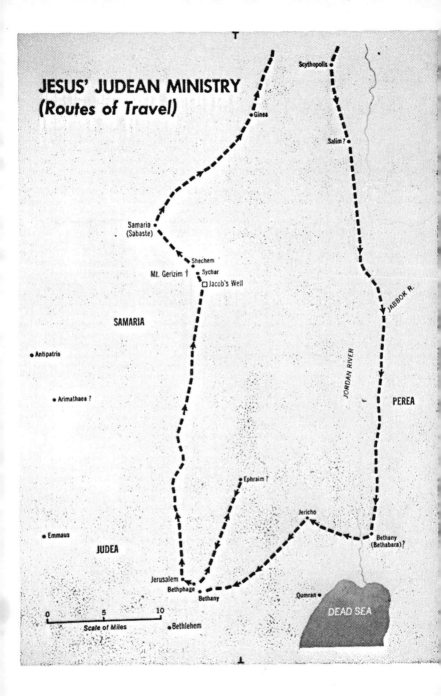

JESUS' JUDEAN MINISTRY
(Routes of Travel)

Scythopolis

Ginea

Salim?

Samaria
(Sabaste)

Shechem

Mt. Gerizim † Sychar
☐ Jacob's Well

SAMARIA

JABBOK R.

• Antipatris

JORDAN RIVER

• Arimathaea ?

PEREA

Ephraim ?

Jericho

• Emmaus

JUDEA

Bethany
(Bethabara)?

Jerusalem
Bethphage
Bethany

Qumran •

DEAD SEA

0   5   10
Scale of Miles

• Bethlehem

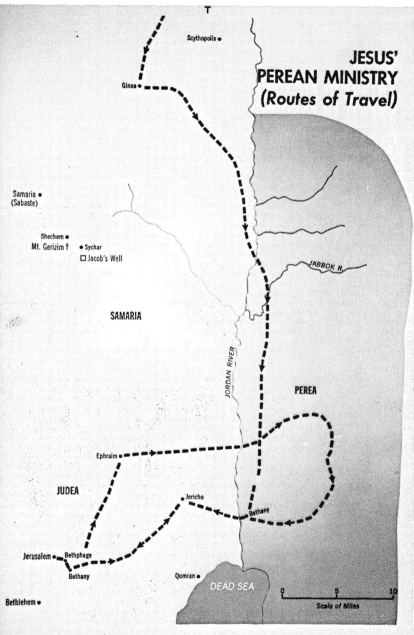

JESUS'
PEREAN MINISTRY
(Routes of Travel)

Scythopolis •

Ginea •

Samaria •
(Sabaste)

Shechem •
Mt. Gerizim †   • Sychar
□ Jacob's Well

JABBOK R.

SAMARIA

JORDAN RIVER

PEREA

Ephraim •

JUDEA

Jericho •

Bethany

Jerusalem •   Bethphage •

Bethany

Qumran •

DEAD SEA

Bethlehem •

0   5   10
Scale of Miles

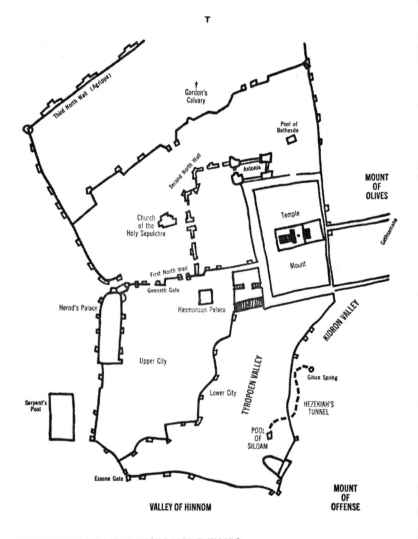

JERUSALEM IN NEW TESTAMENT TIMES